Displays of Affection

by Jean-Jacques Sempé

Translation and introduction
by Edward Koren

D1736584

Workman Publishing, New York

Copyright © 1962, 1964, 1966, 1968, 1970, 1972, 1974, 1975, 1977, 1981 by Jean-Jacques Sempé

All rights reserved. No portion of this book may be reproduced — mechanically, electronically or by any other means, including photocopying — without written permission of the publisher. Published simultaneously in Canada by Saunders of Toronto, Inc.

Library of Congress Cataloging in Publication Data

Sempé, 1932 —
Displays of affection.

1. Love — Caricatures and cartoons. 2. French wit and humor, Pictorial. I. Title.
NC1499.S35A4   1981   741.5'944   81-40504
ISBN 0-89480-194-5 (pbk.)   AACR2

Book design: Florence Cassen Mayers

Workman Publishing Company, Inc.
1 West 39 Street
New York, New York 10018

Manufactured in the United States of America
First printing September 1981
10   9   8   7   6   5   4   3   2   1

The success of a social satirist can be measured by how much enthusiasm for his work the subjects (and objects) of his satire are willing to show. The great popularity in France enjoyed by Sempé attests to the fond way the French have come to view themselves through his eyes and ears, and to rely on his extraordinary sensibility to get an original view of themselves. He has become the contemporary bearer of Daumier's keen vision, but in a way that transcends the boundaries of his native country. The people in Sempé's world are more the denizens of a worldwide *petite bourgeoisie,* equally identifiable in both hemispheres and on all the inhabited continents. They live in the humdrum shadow of greatness that for them is chronically out of reach. Inspiration, passion, joy, immortality are some of the ideals never achieved by Sempé's people, who must content themselves with mundane issues of sustenance, security, uncertainty, anxiety, anger, timidity, and self-importance, to name but a few. All this (and many more subtle and sensitive ingredients) is made laughable and sad by Sempé, who mixes his people into situations that are clichés of modern life everywhere.

Displays of Affection has Sempé fixing his voyeuristic eye and eavesdropping ear on that most clichéd of all subjects — relationships. The great ideal of the grand and lasting passion smiles down on the bumbling solitude of his lovers and mates, who fight, scold, daydream, protect themselves with envelopes of self-importance, always ending up in the same routinized lives they started with. And what is amazing to those of us enmeshed in the deadly seriousness of these matters is how Sempé, with Olympian dispassion, makes it all familiar, personal, real, and truly funny. He is the master of observed comic detail — the comfortable decor, the enormously complex interior environment, the flamboyant gesture or anguished throw of the body. His small people in huge surrounding spaces is a kind of shorthand to set all of this in perspective, and their intense, self involvement and seriousness is what makes us laugh and see it all a little more clearly. *Displays of Affection* is for Sempé a display of love — for his people, who are — like us — as vulnerable and lovable as they are laughable.

Edward Koren

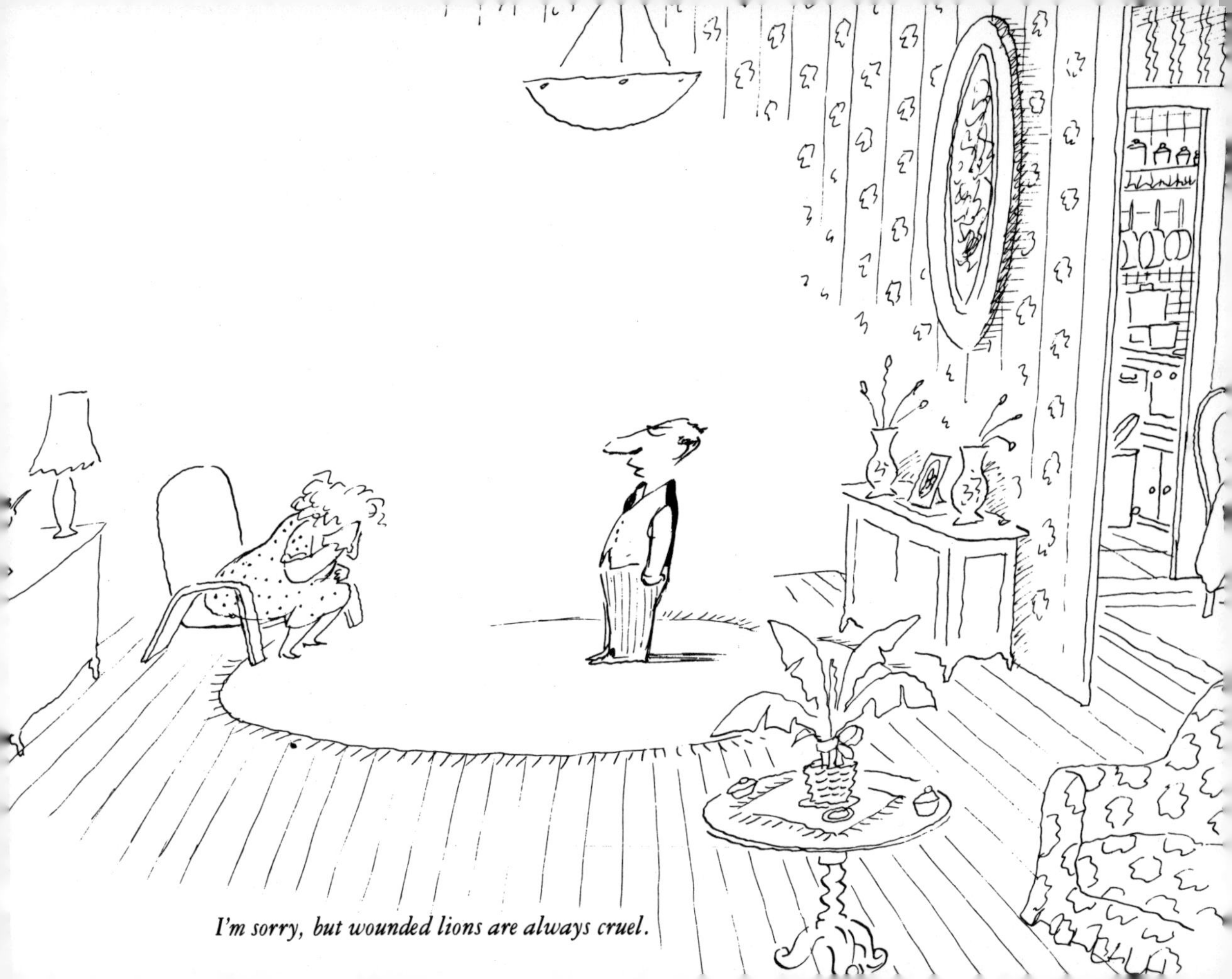

I'm sorry, but wounded lions are always cruel.

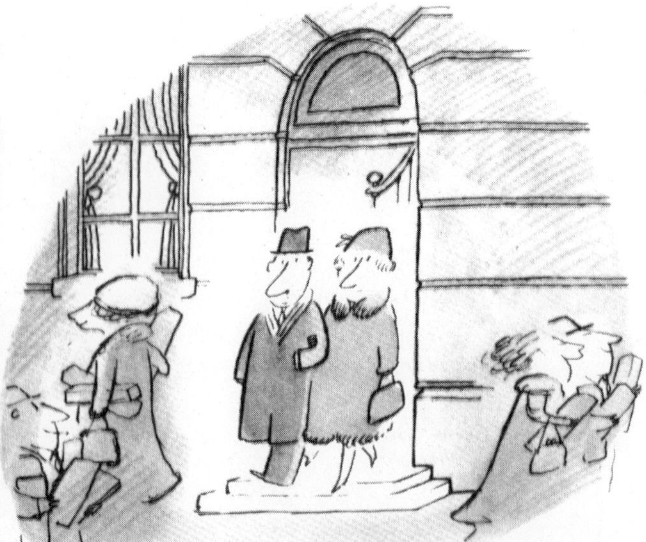

1

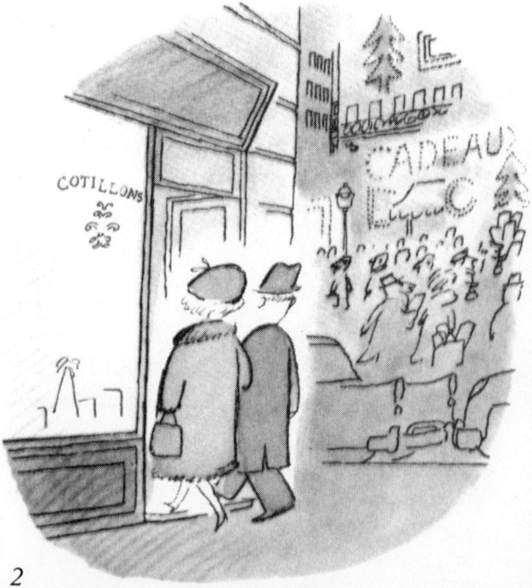
COTILLONS
CADEAU

2

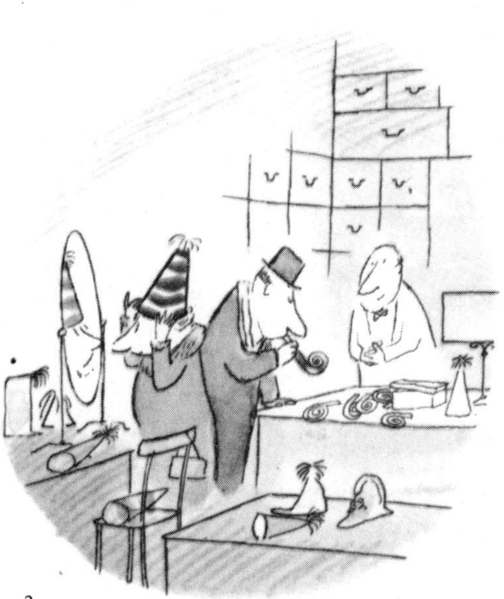

3

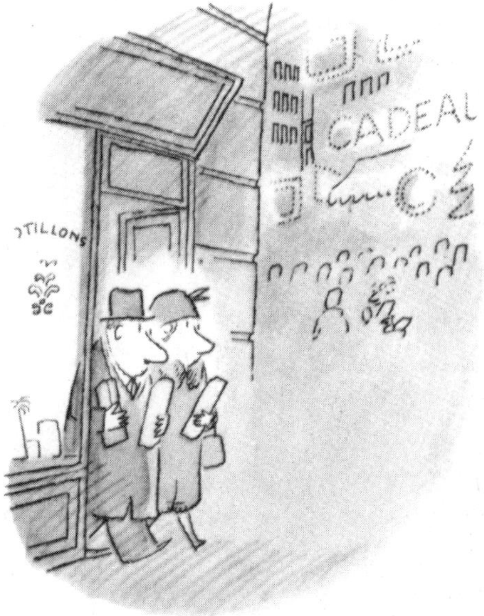
TILLONS
CADEAU

4

5

6

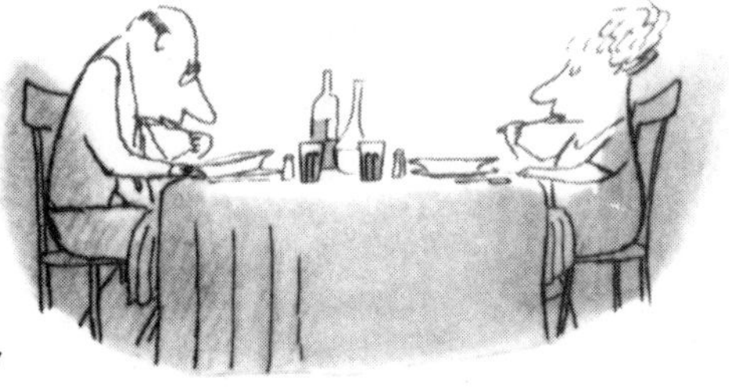

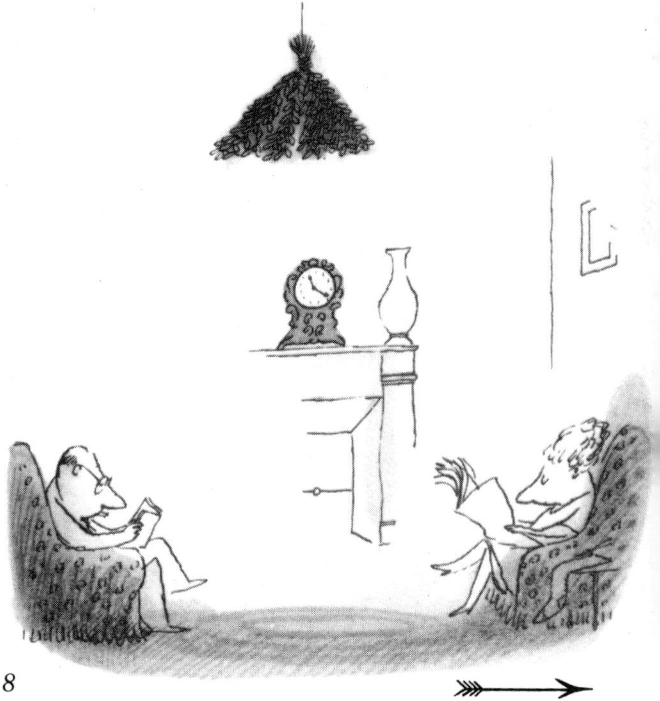

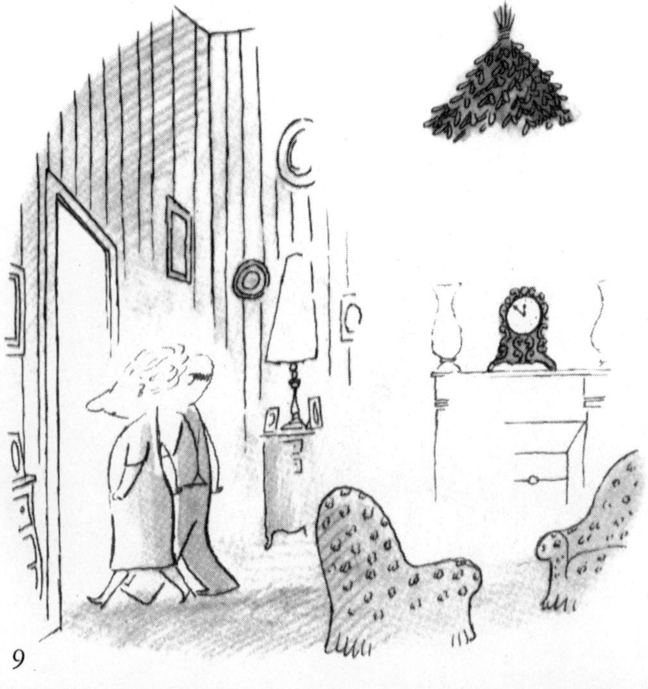

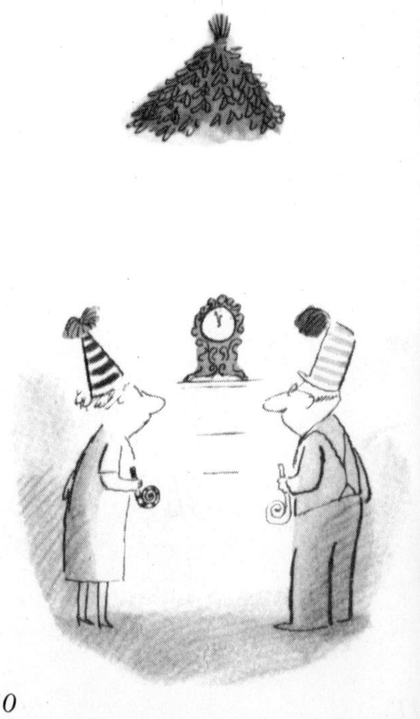

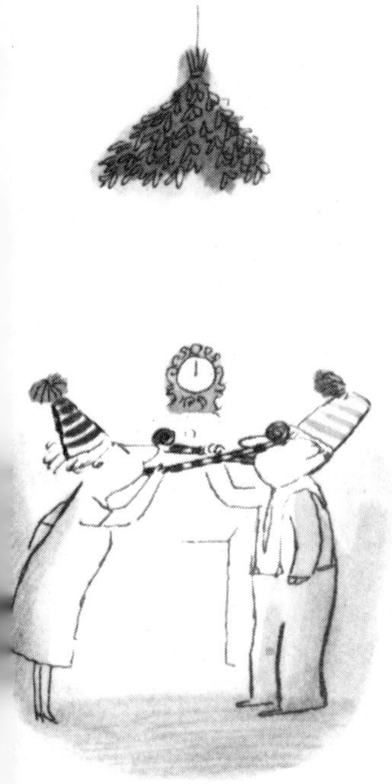

11

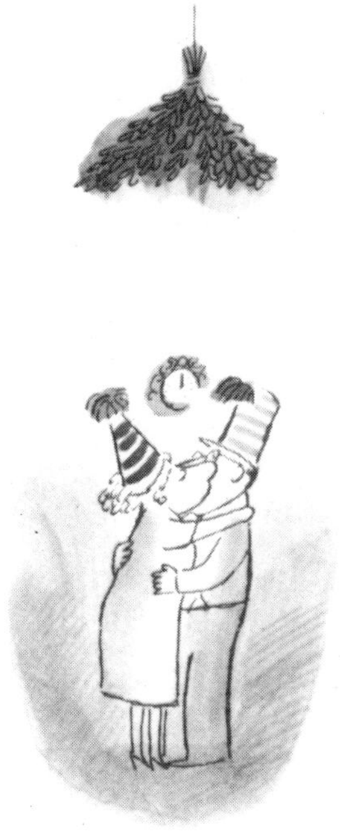

12

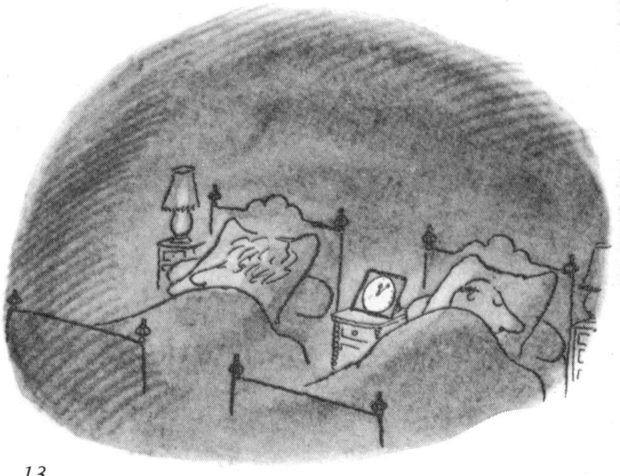

13

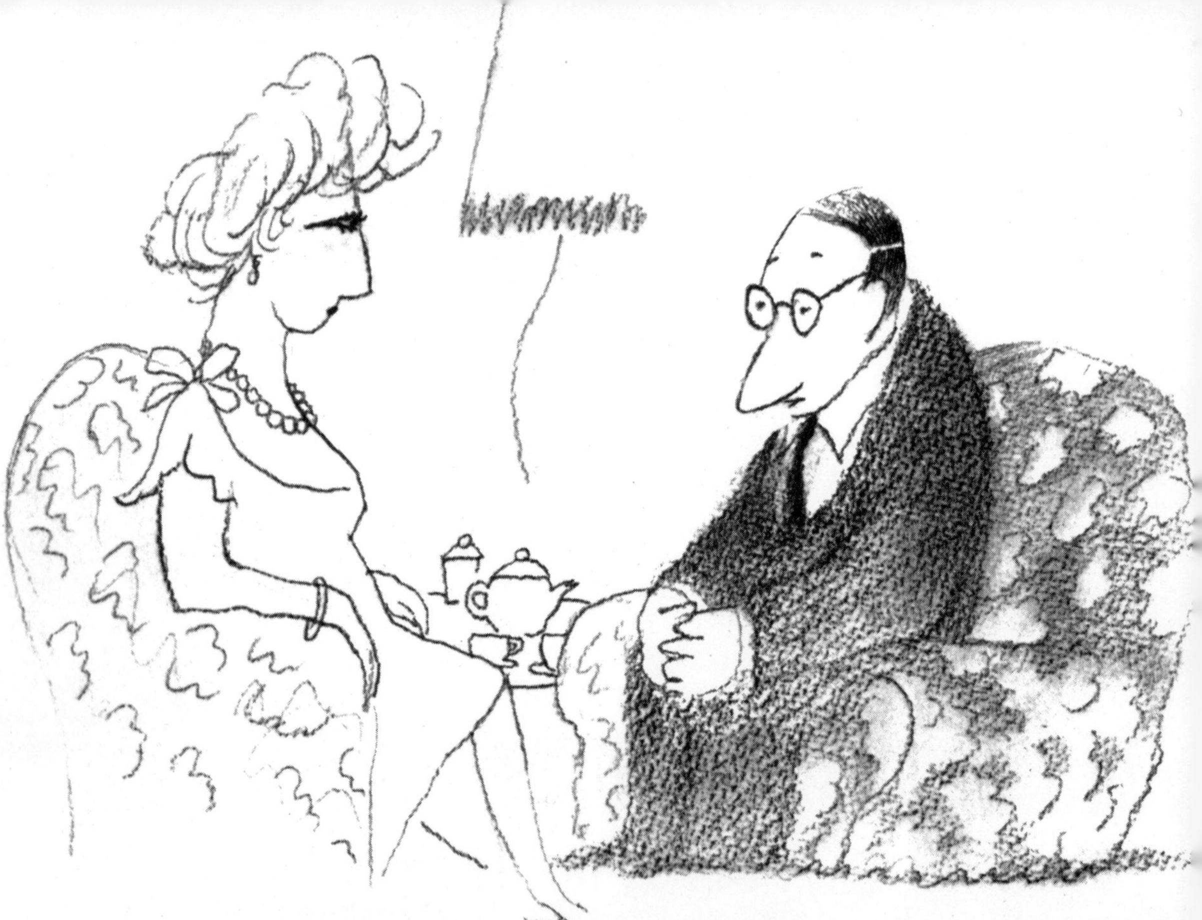

Irene, you've got to accept the reality that my presence in your life would be only that of a meteor.

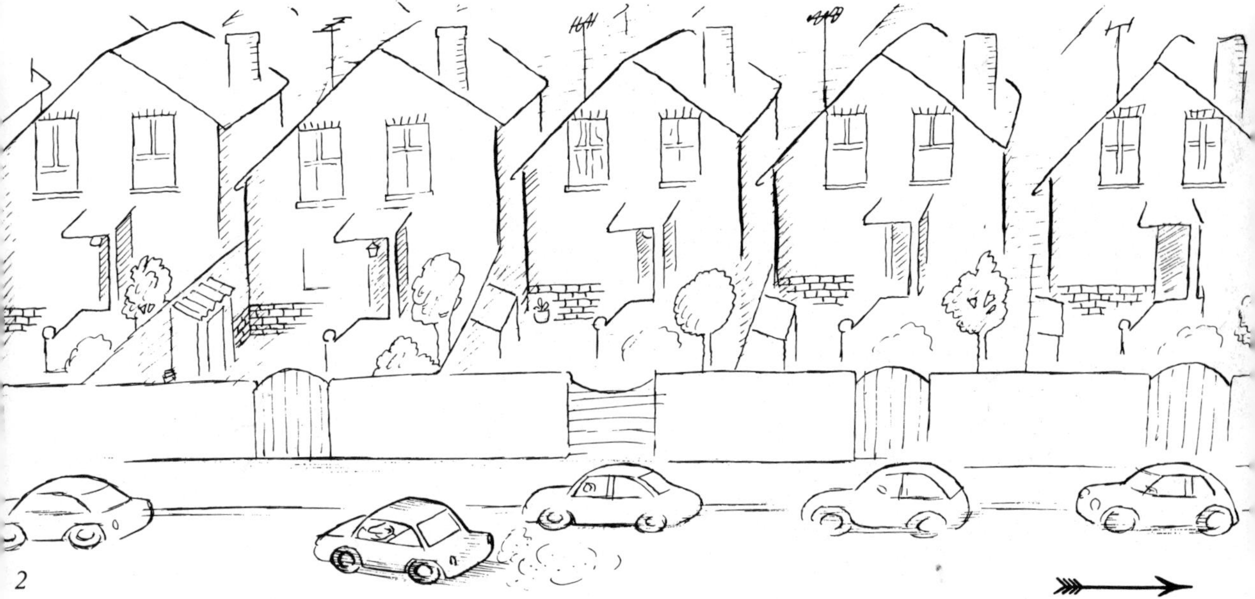

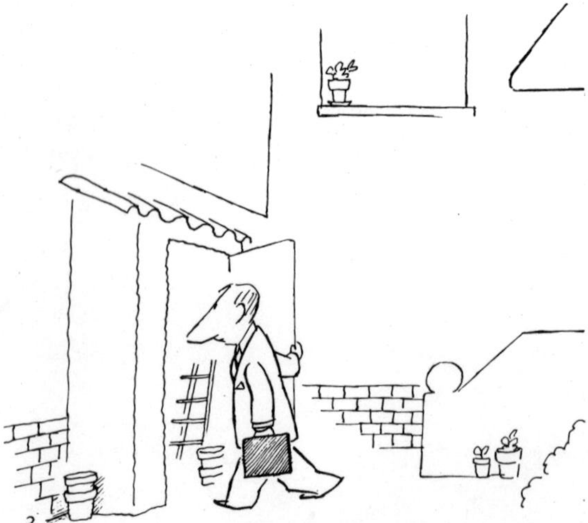

3

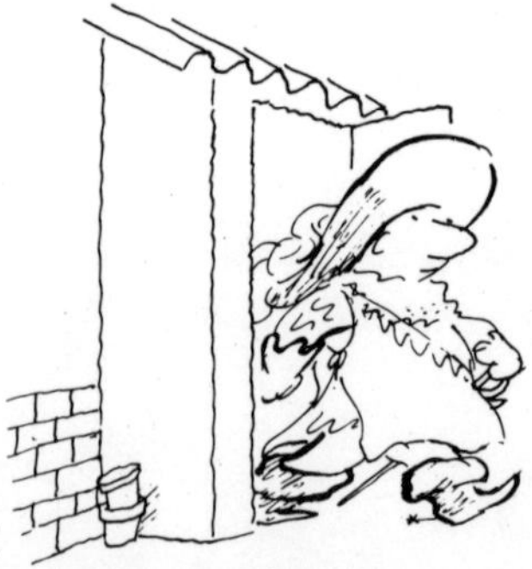

4

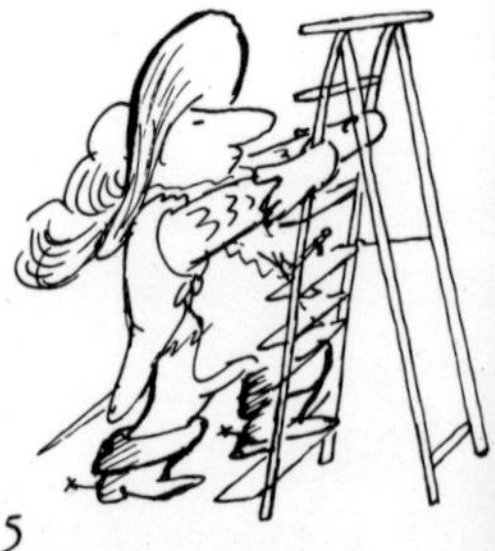

5

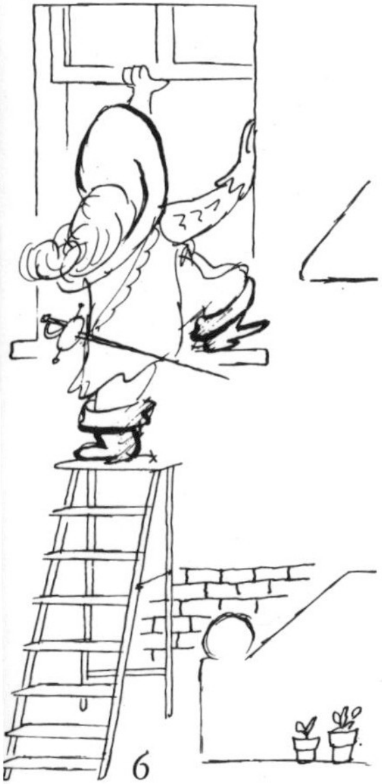

6

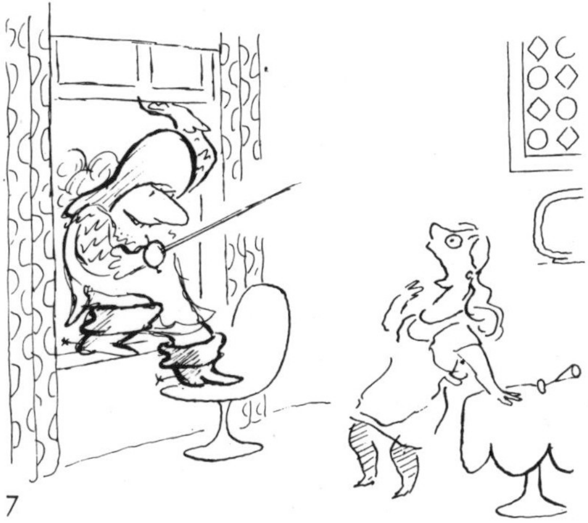

7

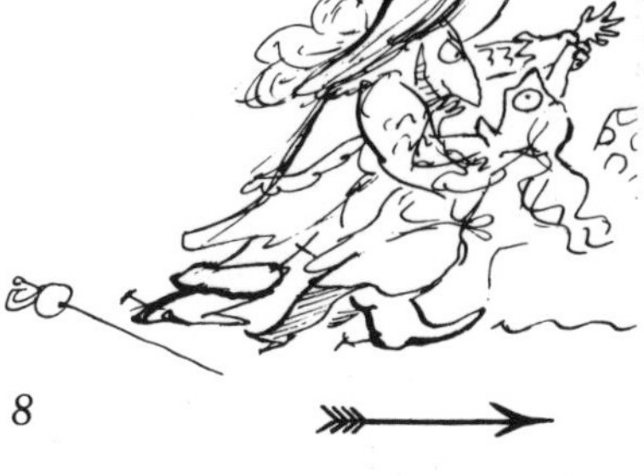

8

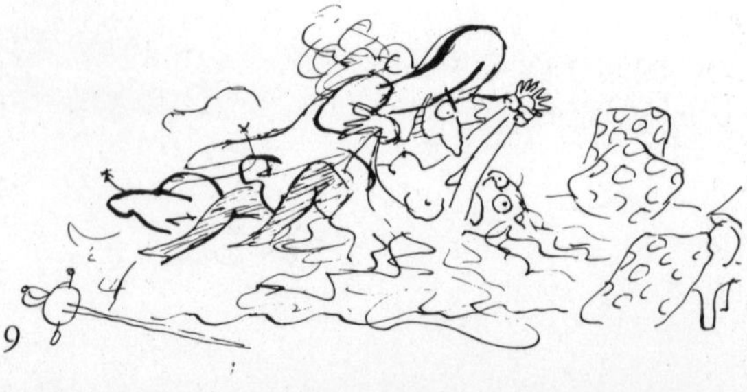

9

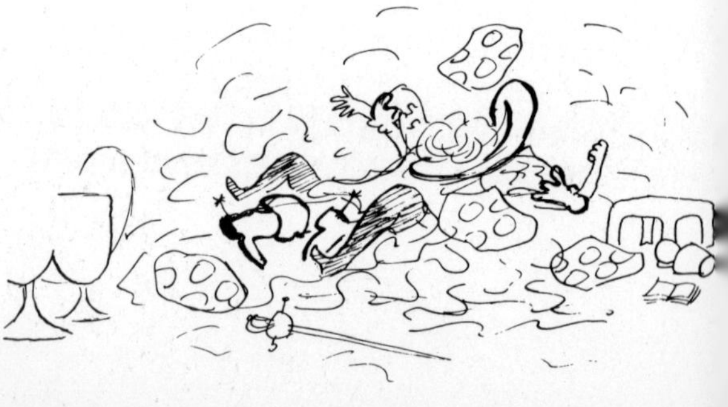

10

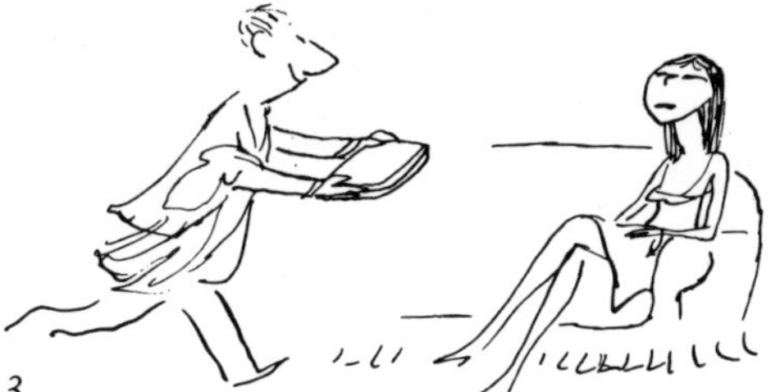

3

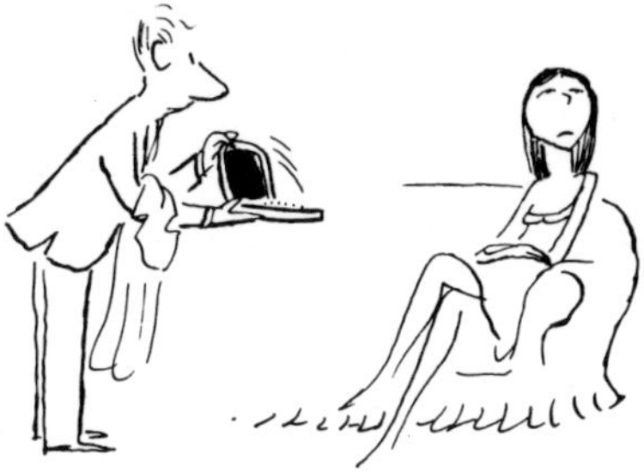

4

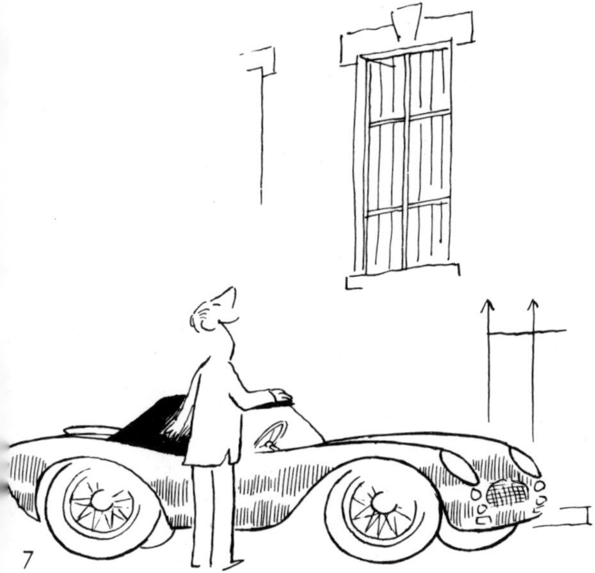

7

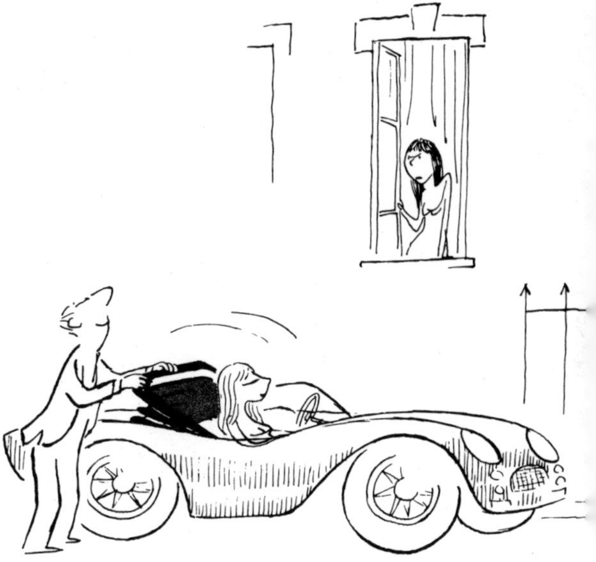

8

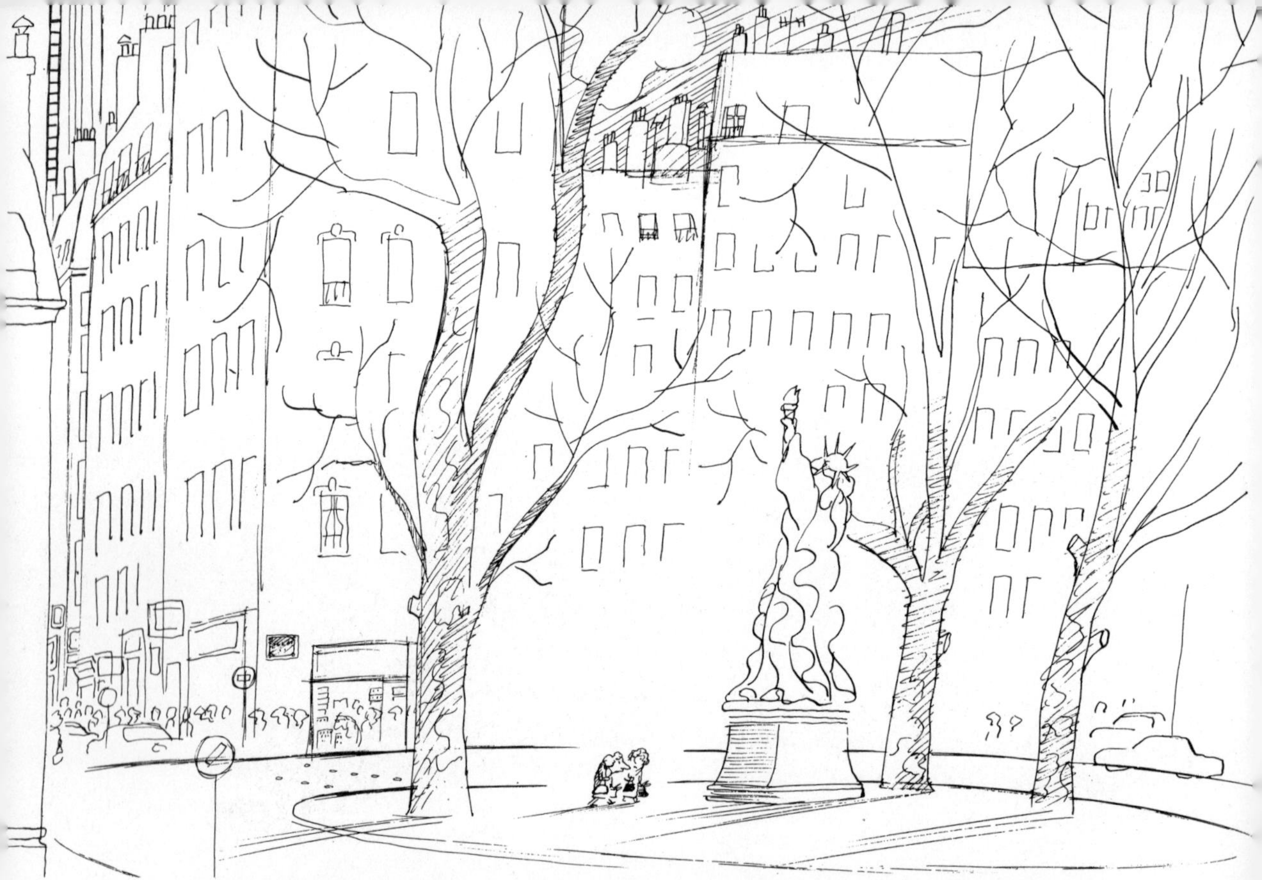

Only once did I ever allow myself to be swept away by passion, and the next day there was a plague of locusts in the south and the Andrea Doria *sank.*

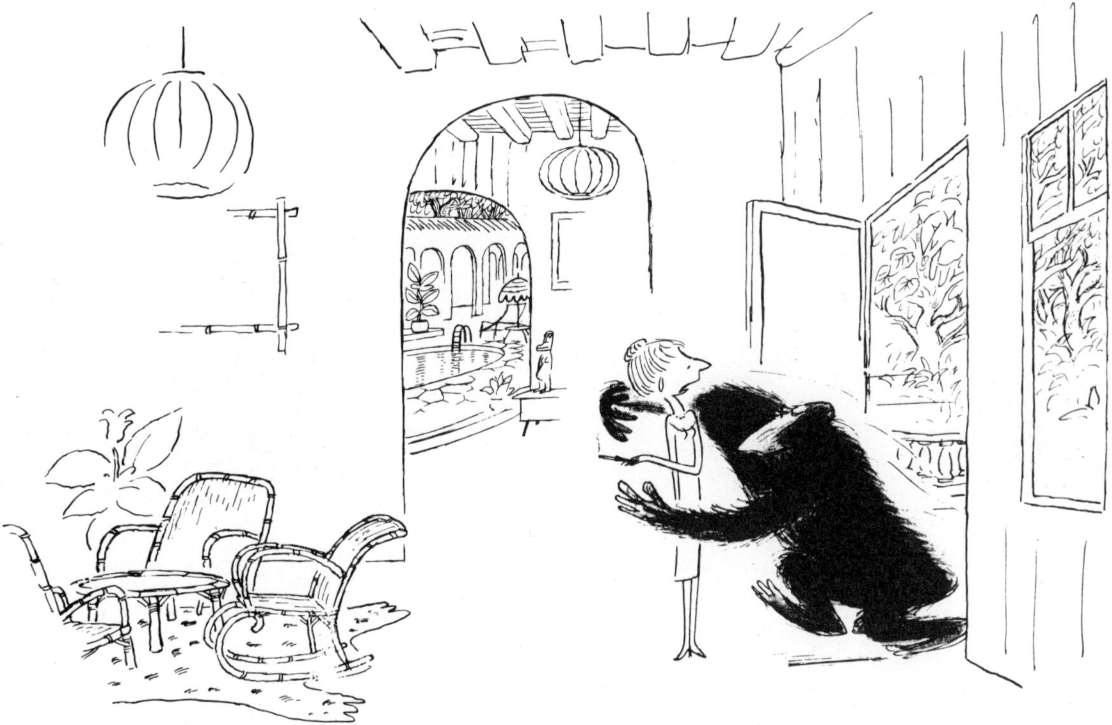

What on earth has gotten into you? Are you drunk?

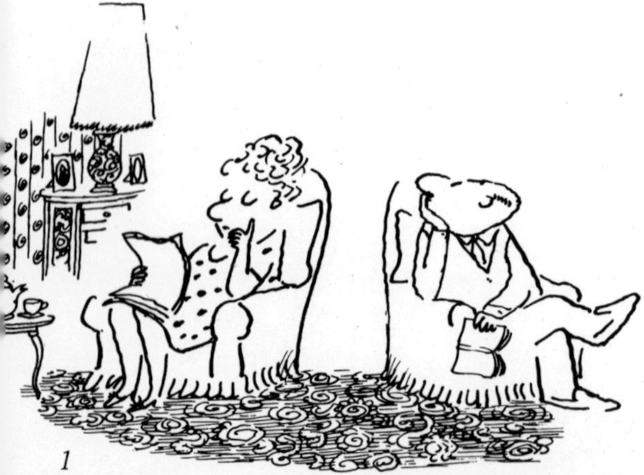

1

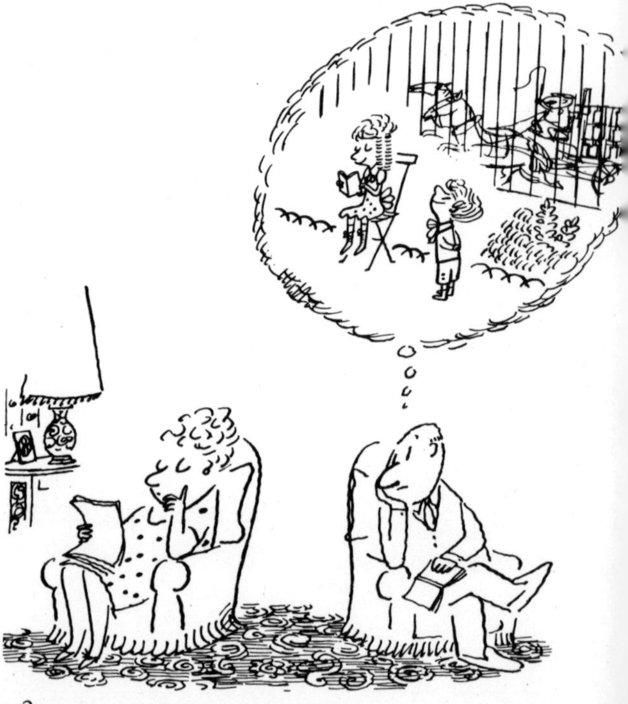

2

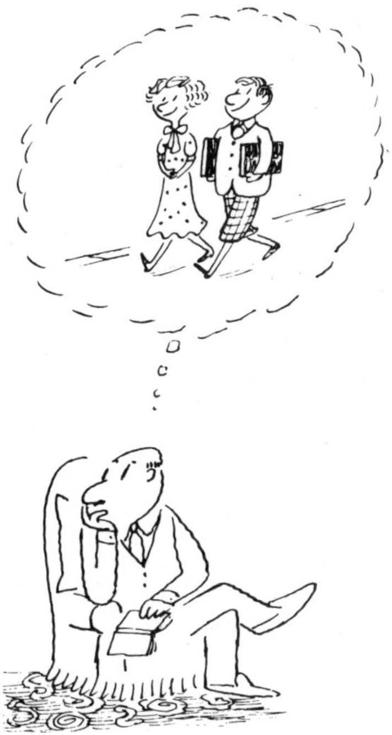

3

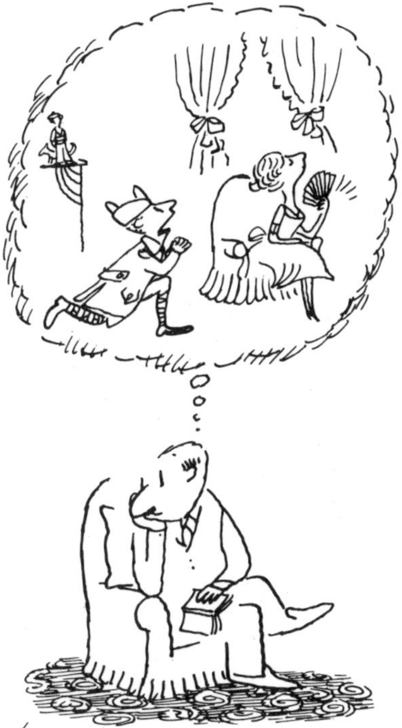

4

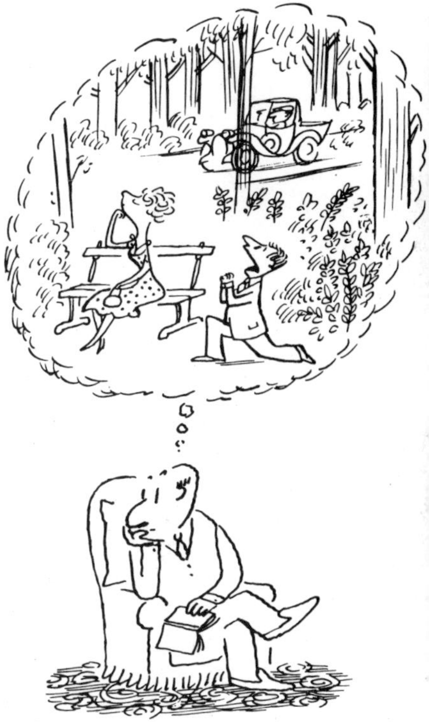

5

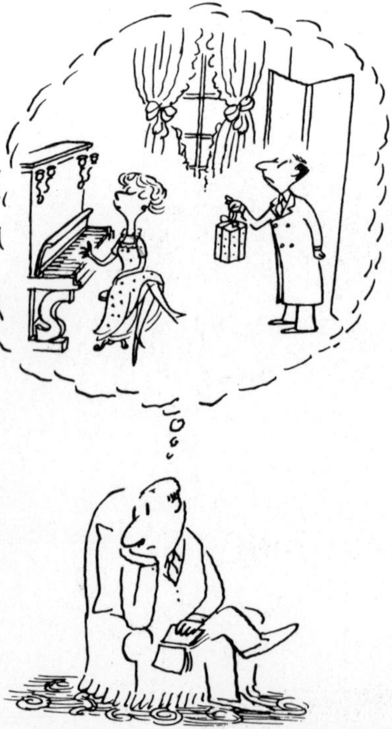

6

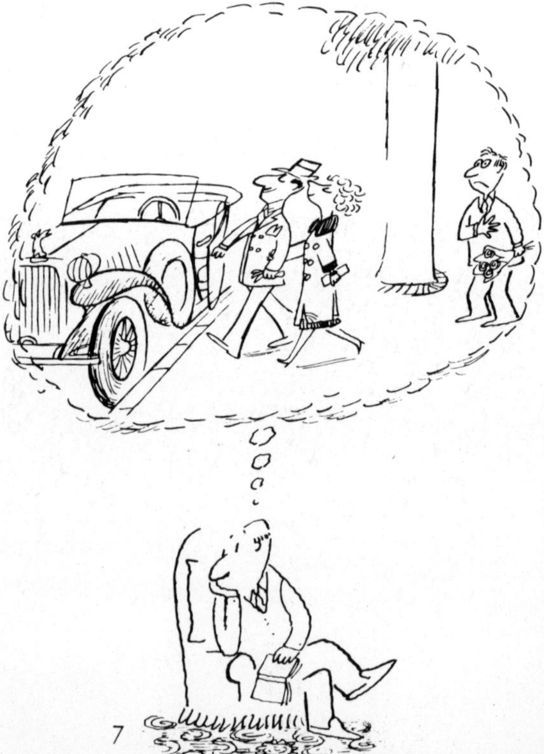

7

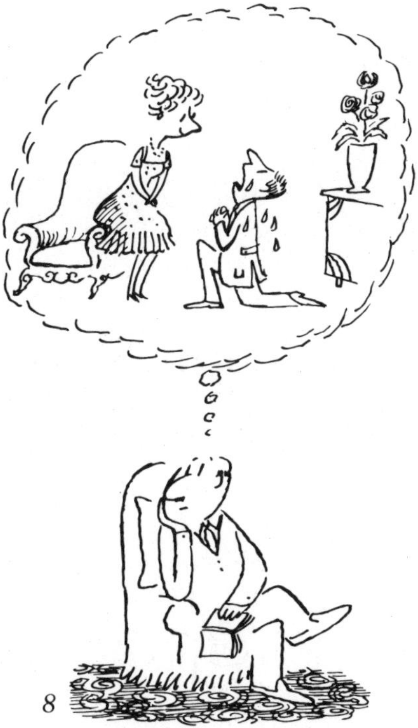

8

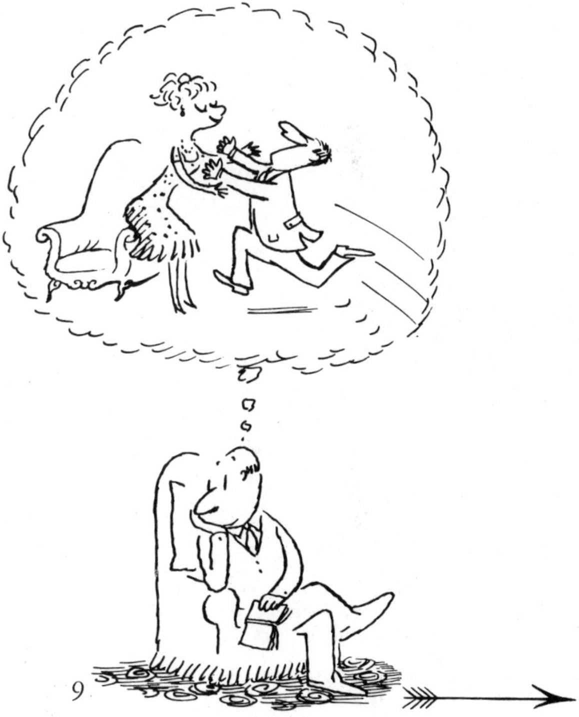

9

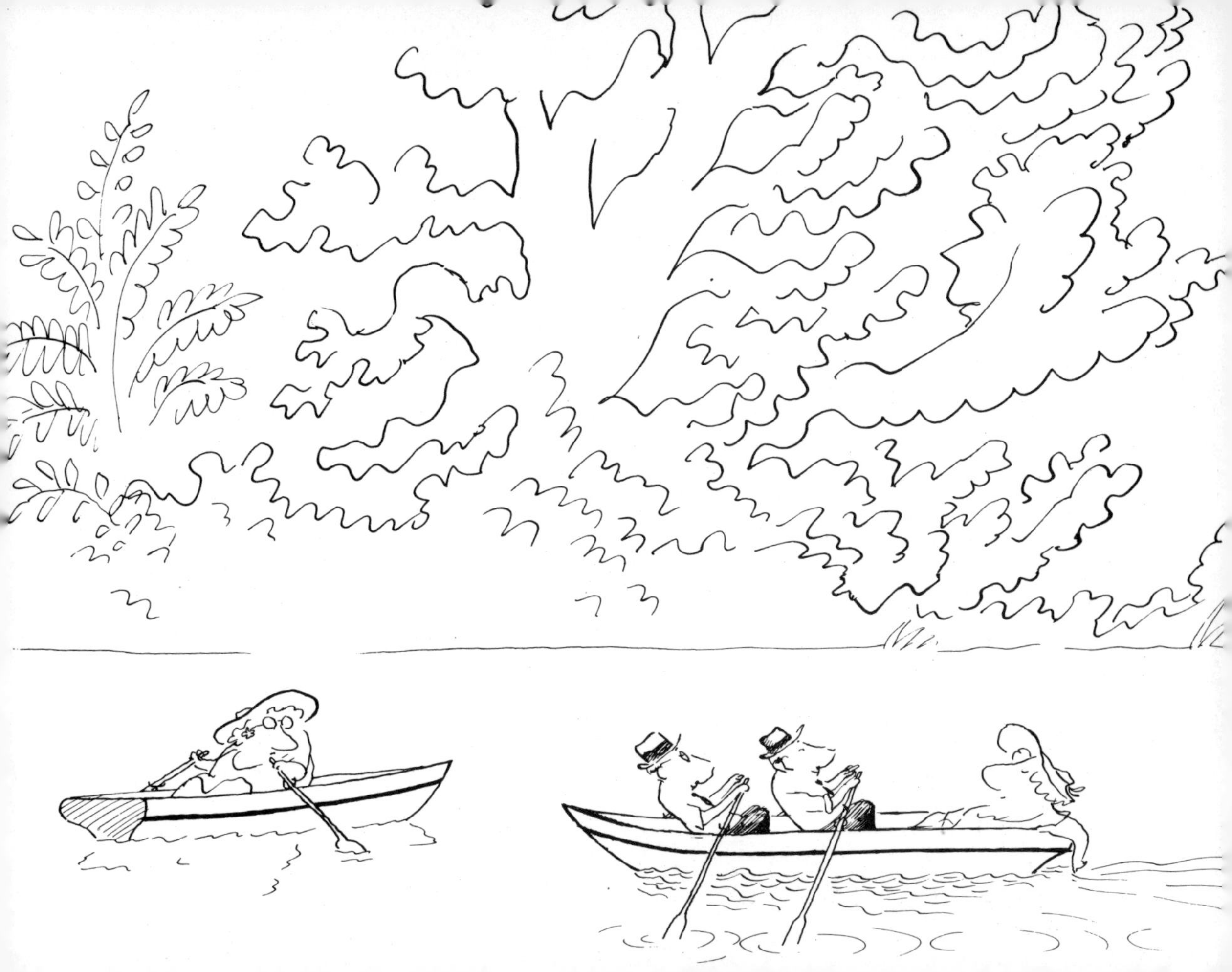

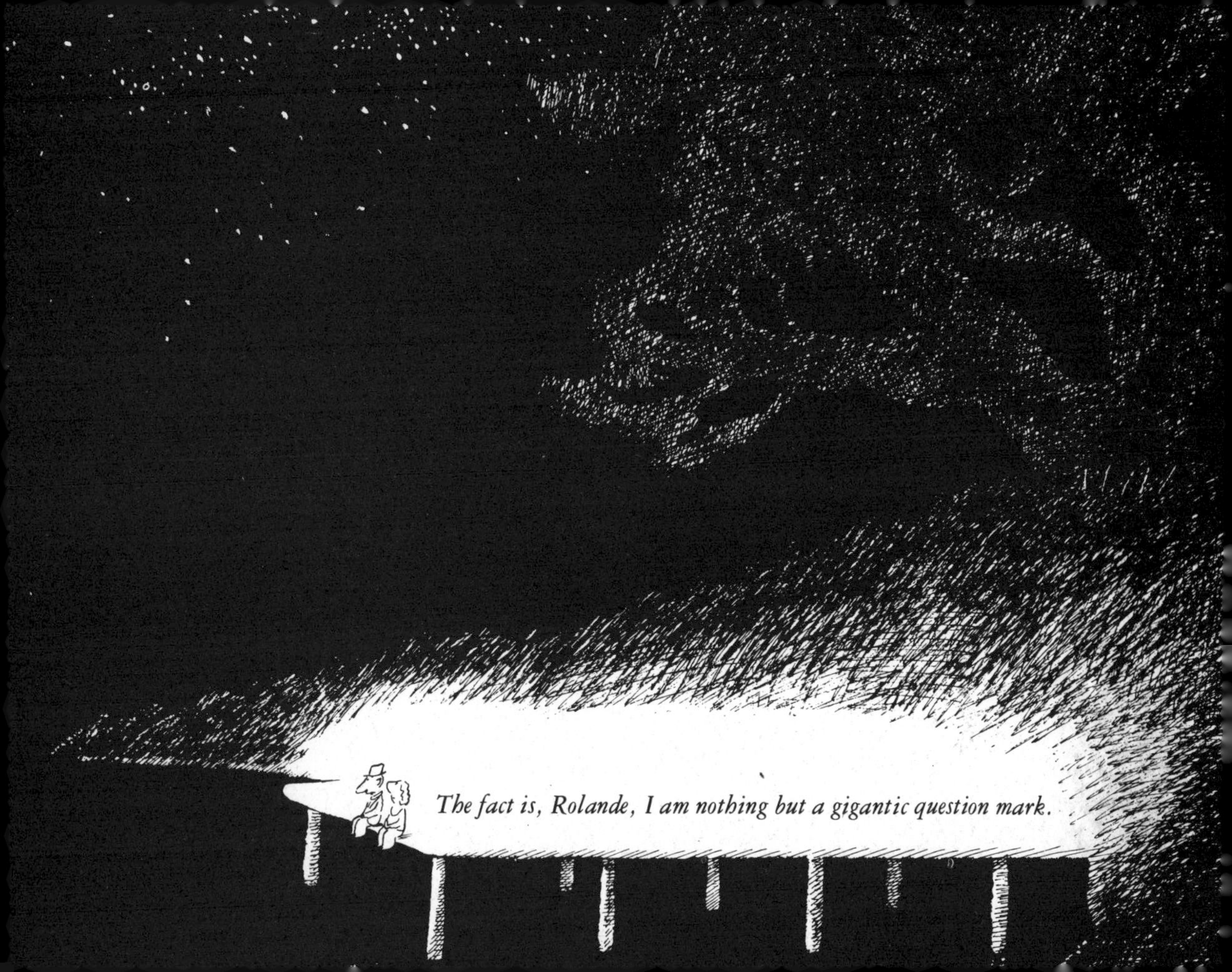

The fact is, Rolande, I am nothing but a gigantic question mark.

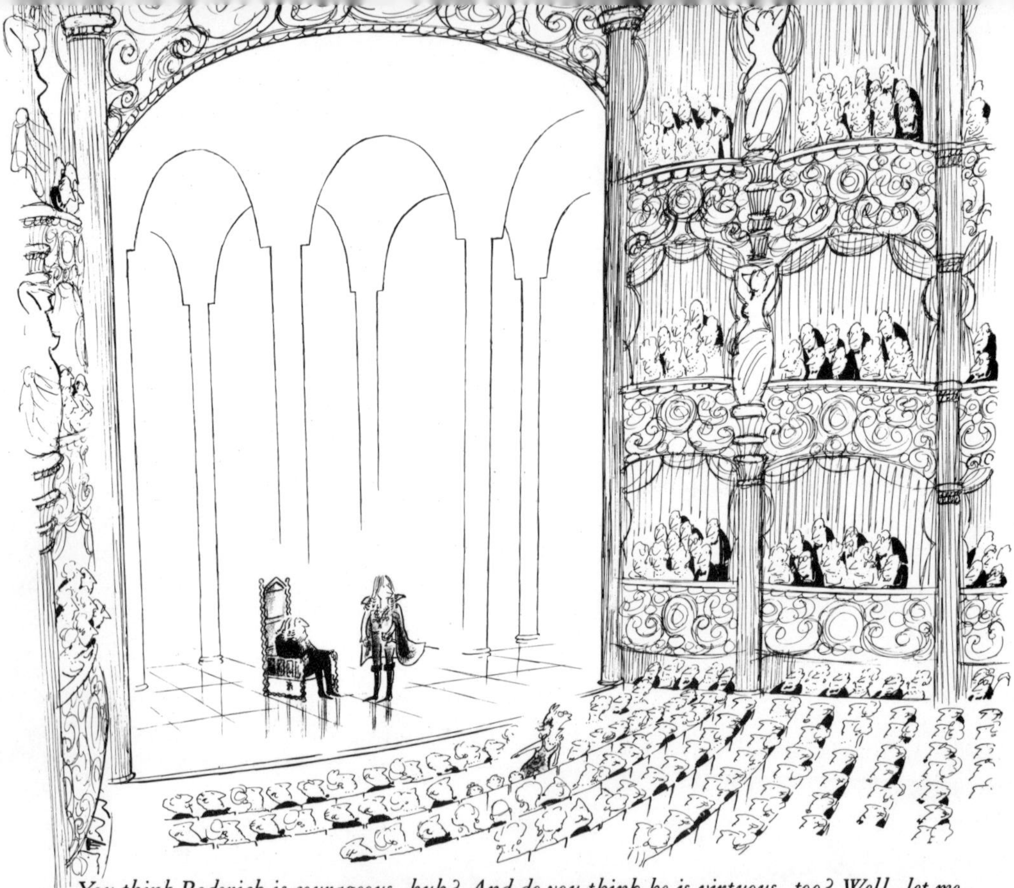

You think Roderick is courageous, huh? And do you think he is virtuous, too? Well, let me just tell you how much alimony and child support he gives me and the children.

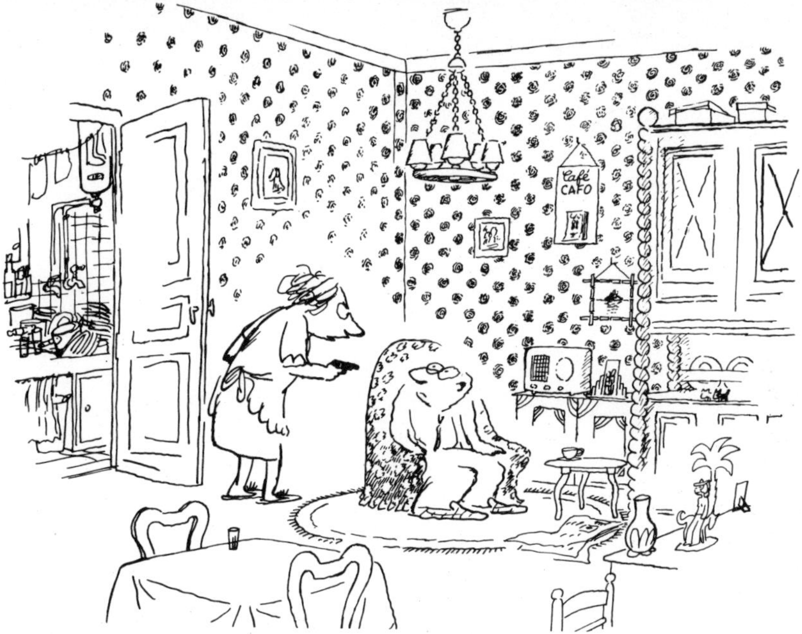
Café
CAFO

It would have been wonderful if you were a poor and sick artist when I met you. I would have taken care of you. I would have helped you all that I possibly could. We would have had discouraging times but we would have had wonderful ones, too. To the best of my powers, I would have protected you from the daily problems of life so that you could devote yourself completely to your art. And little by little you'd become known. You would have become a great artist, admired, respected, adored; and one day you would have left me for a younger and prettier woman. It's for that *that I'll never forgive you.*

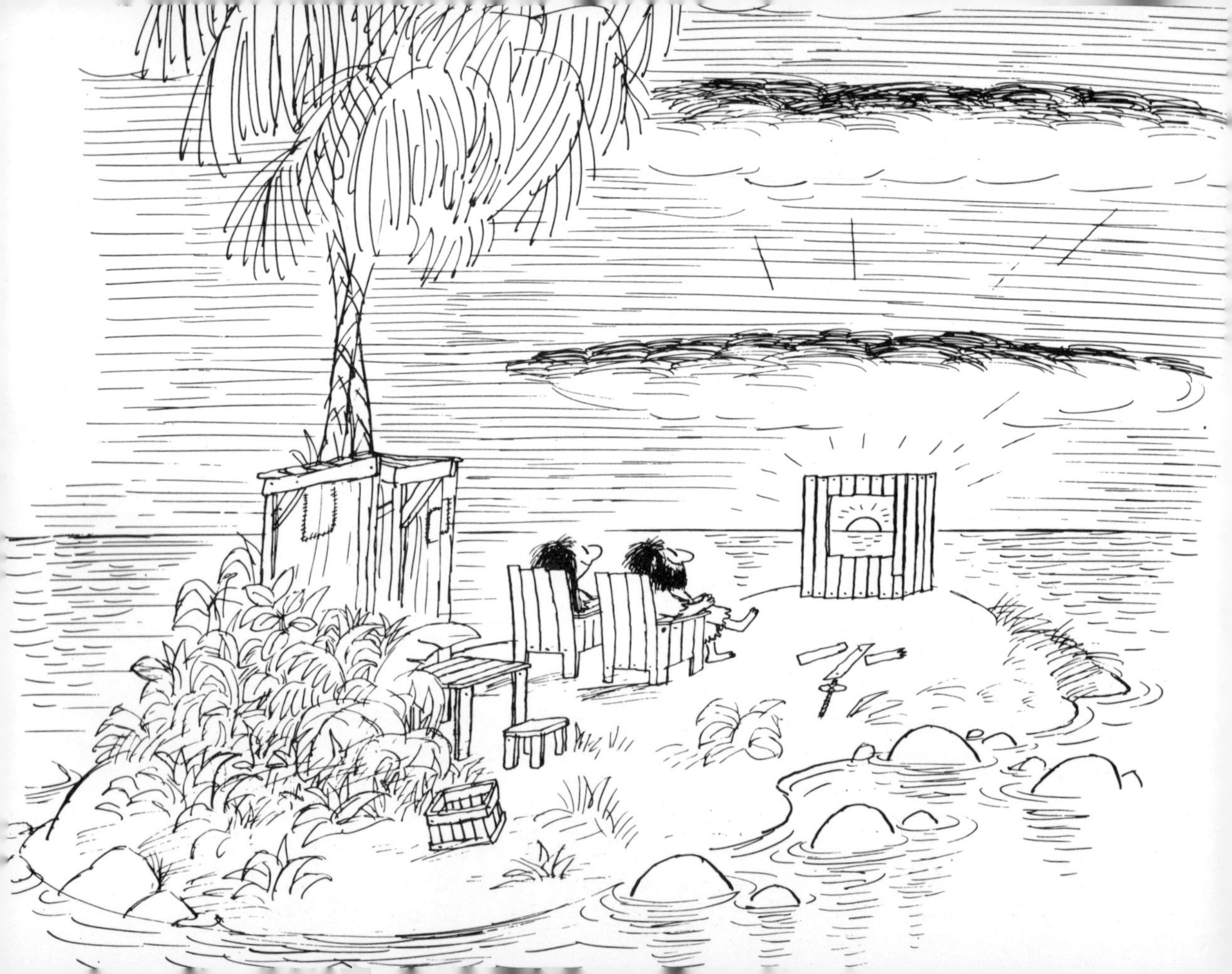

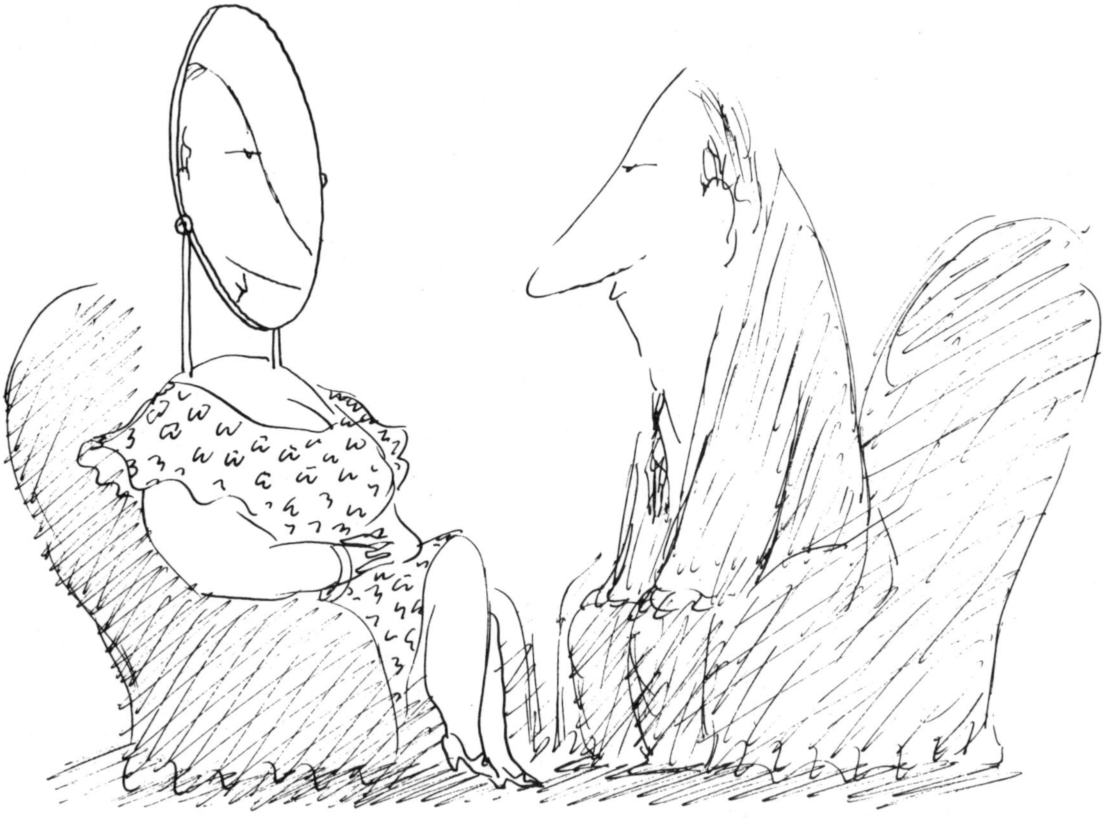

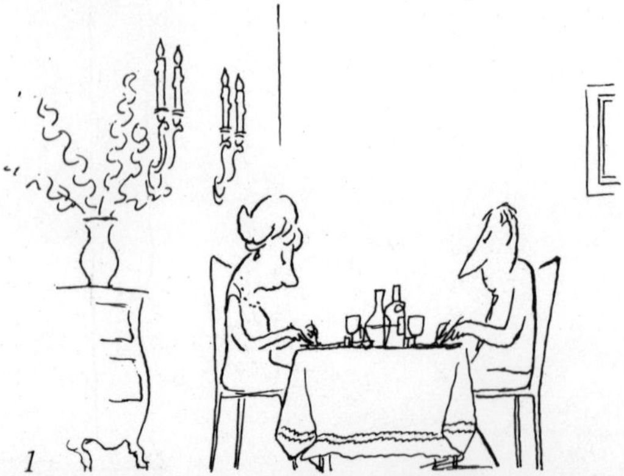

1

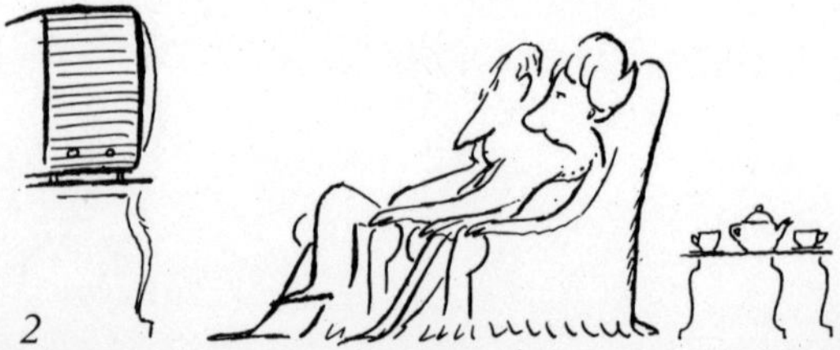

2

3

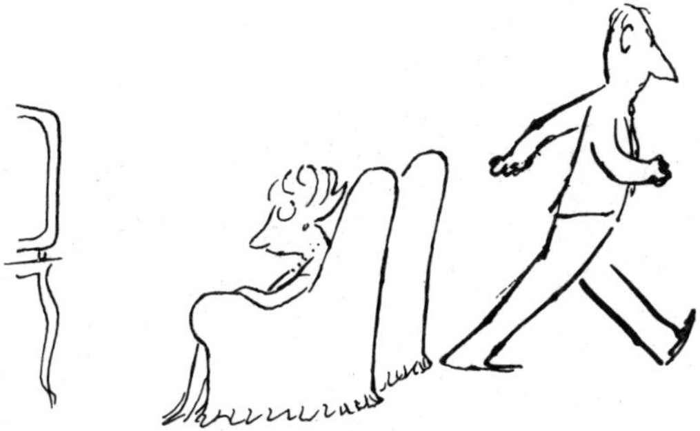

4

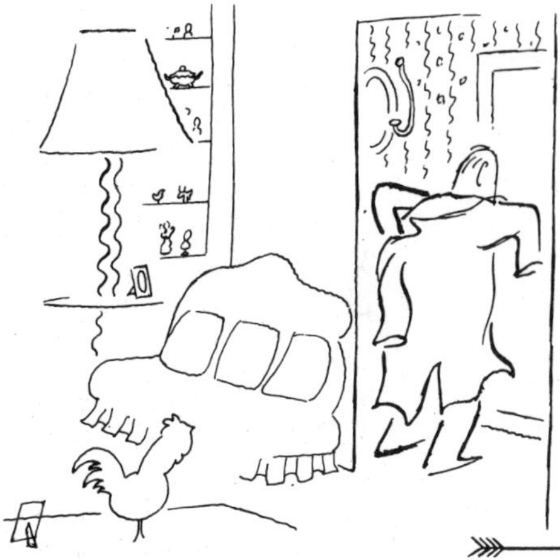

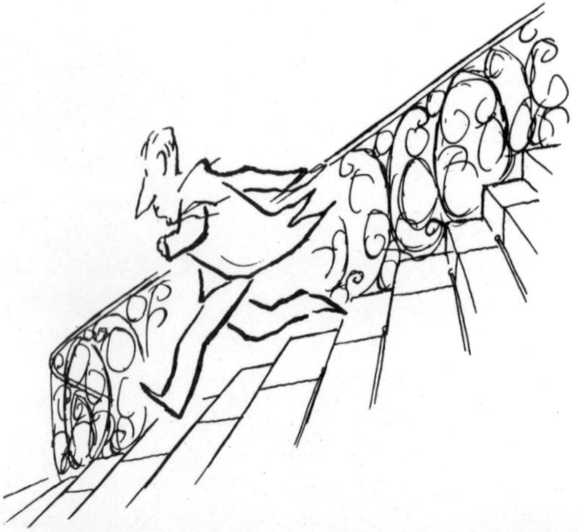

5

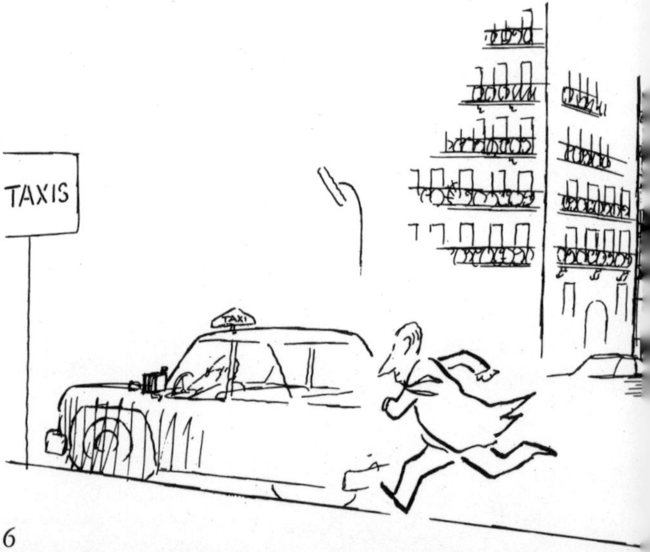
TAXIS
TAXI

6

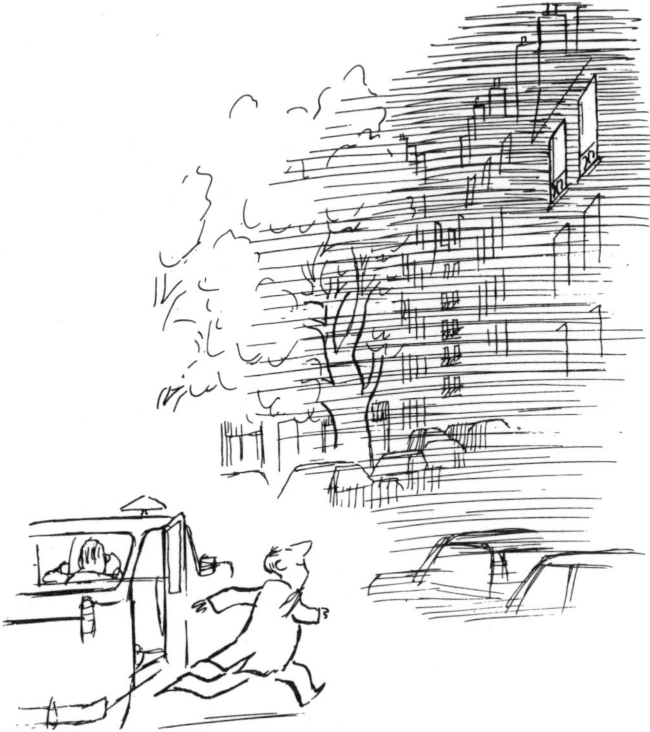

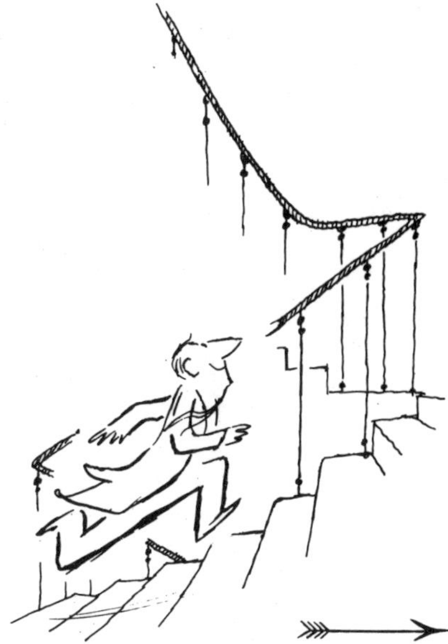

9

10

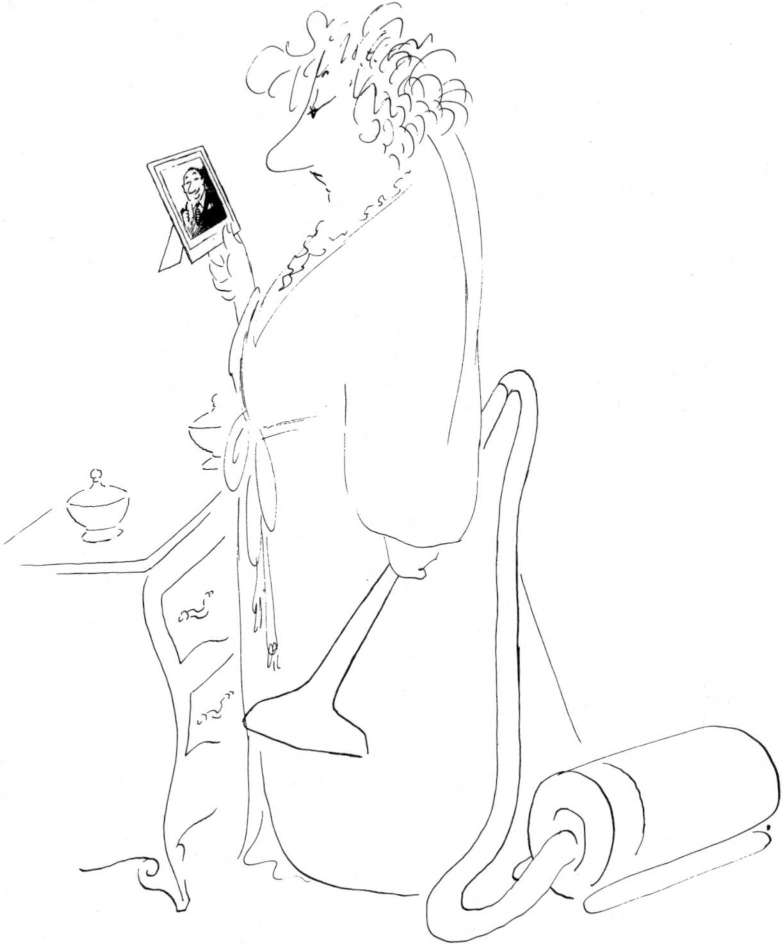

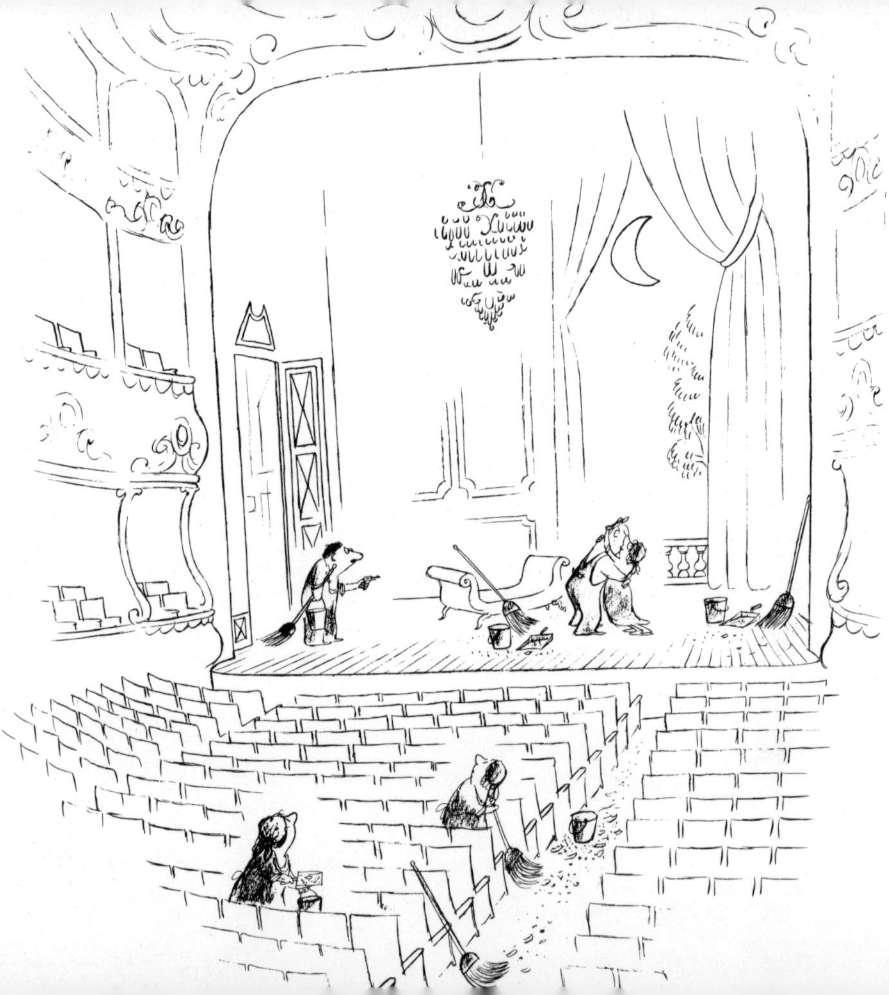

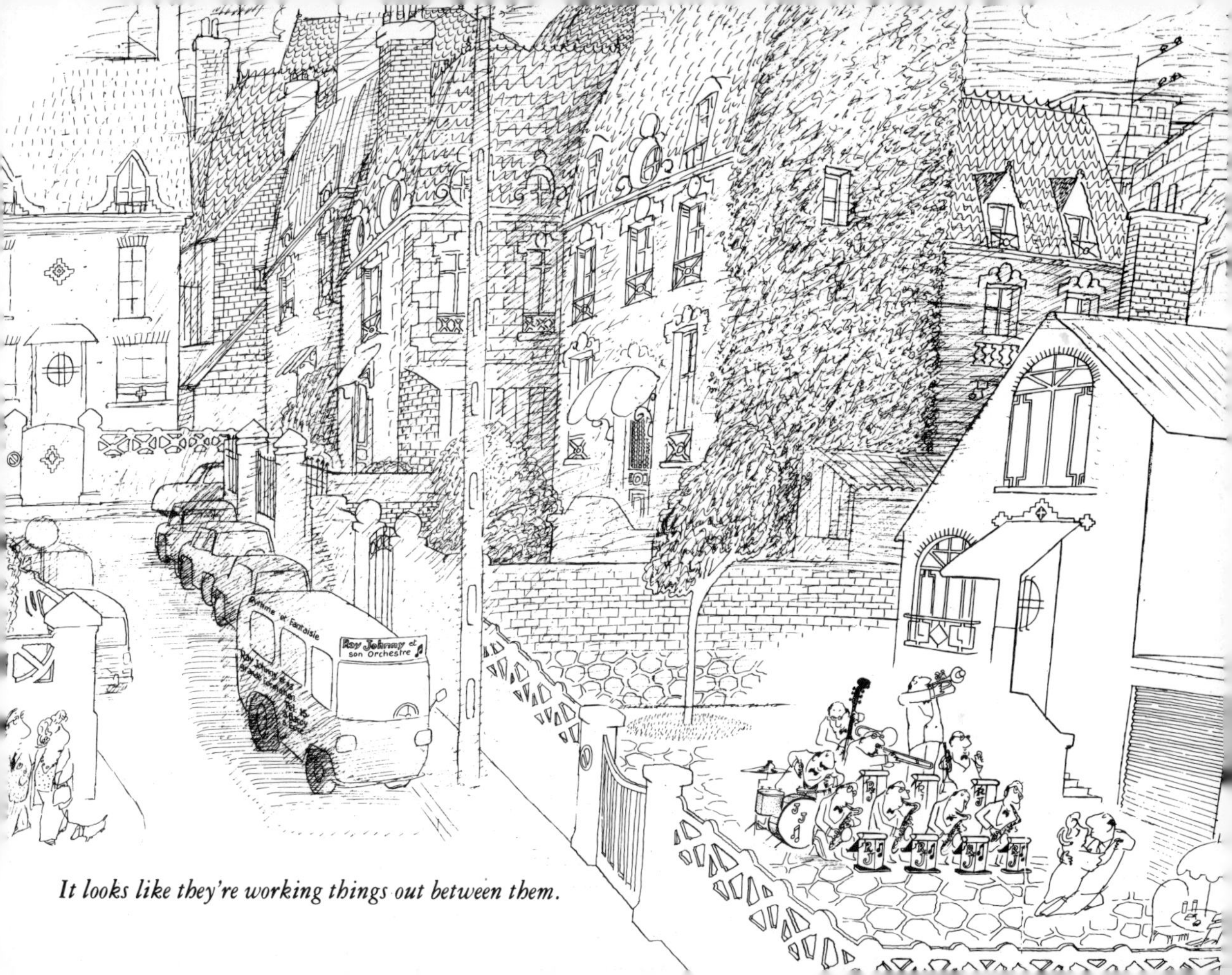
Rythme et Fantaisie
Ray Johnny et son Orchestre

It looks like they're working things out between them.

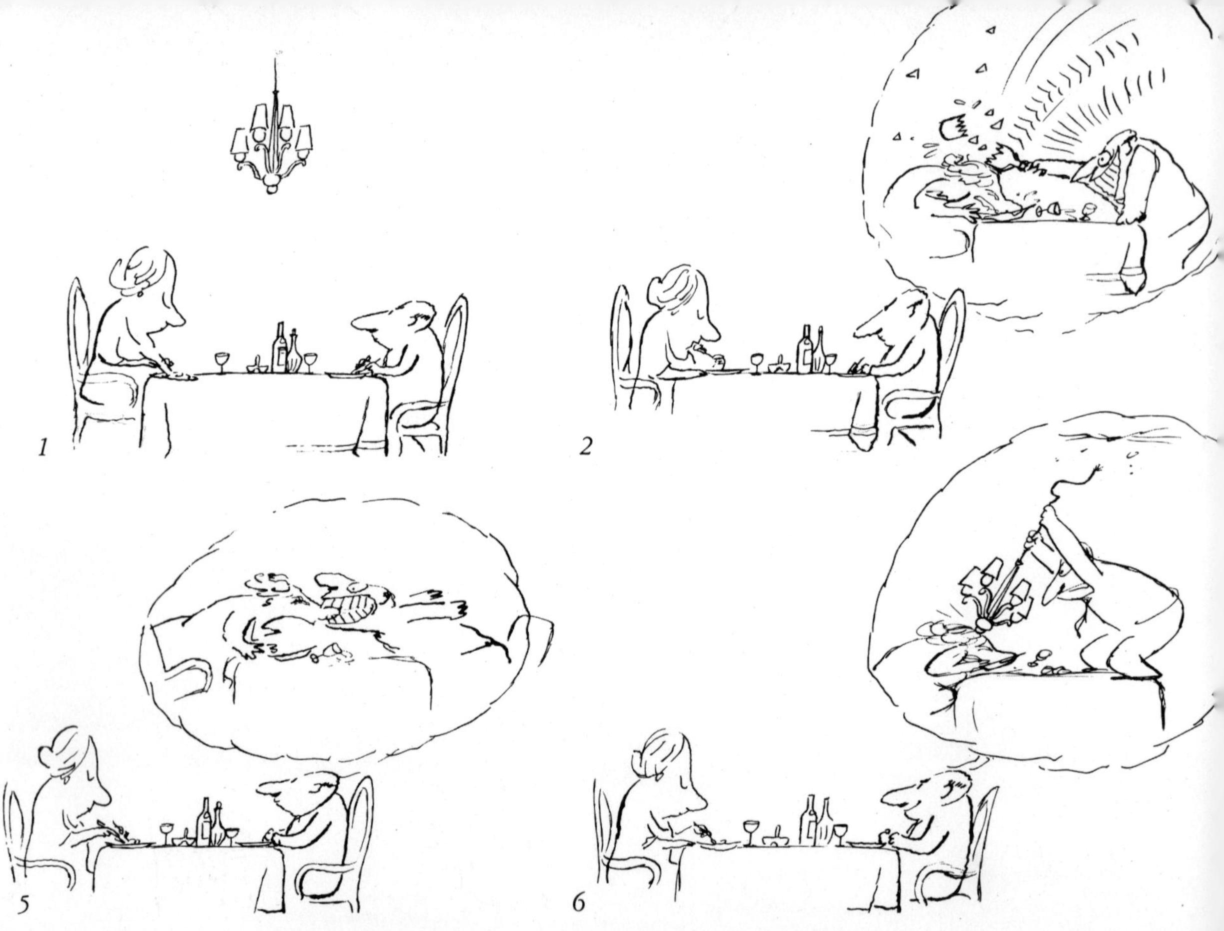
1
2
5
6

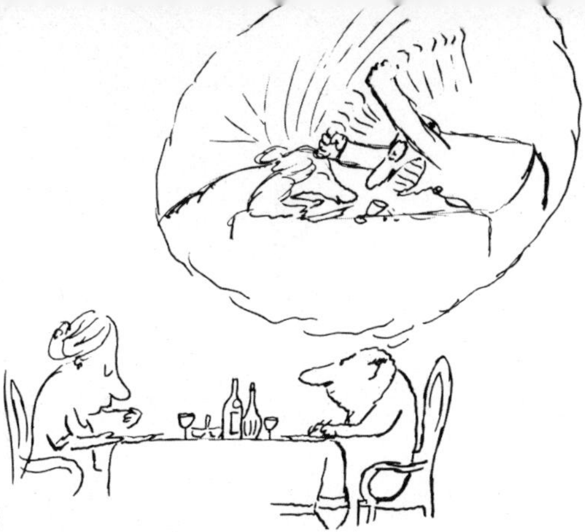

3

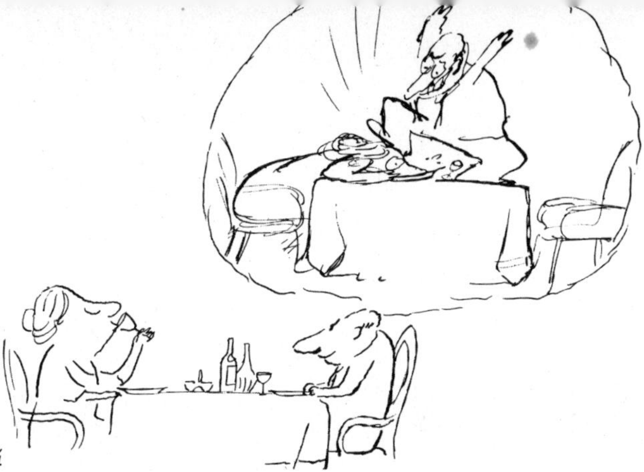

4

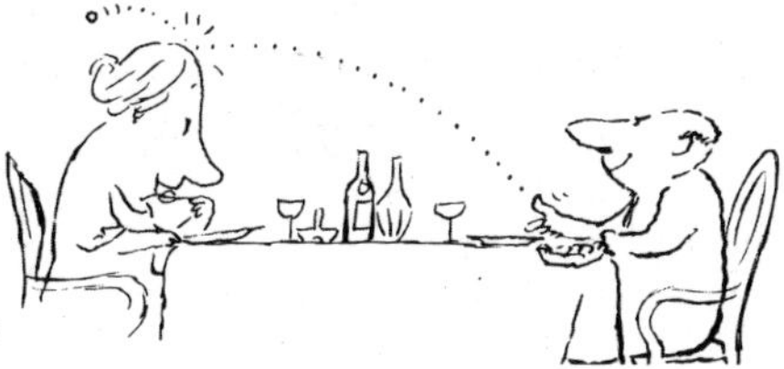

7

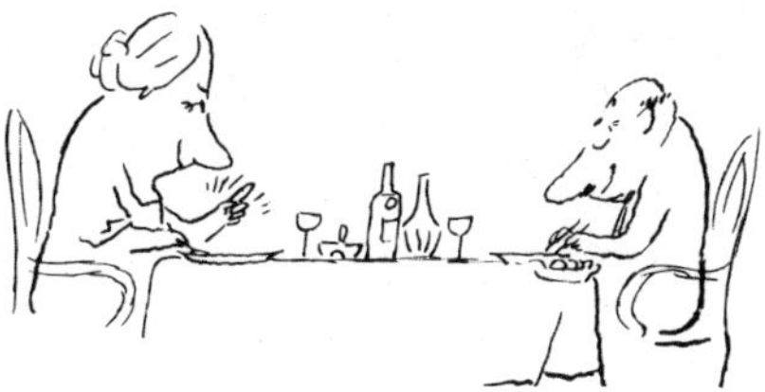

8

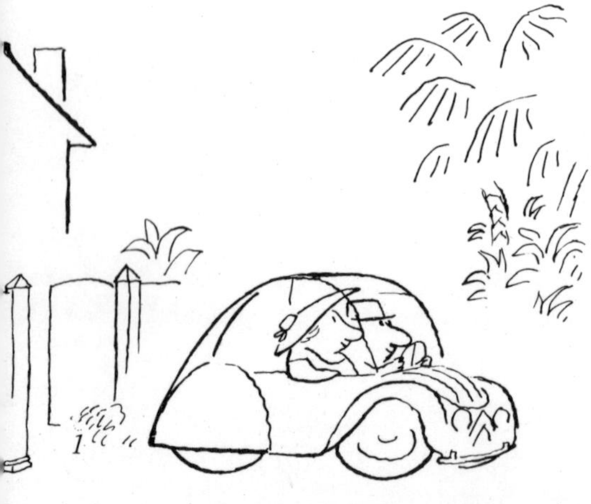

1

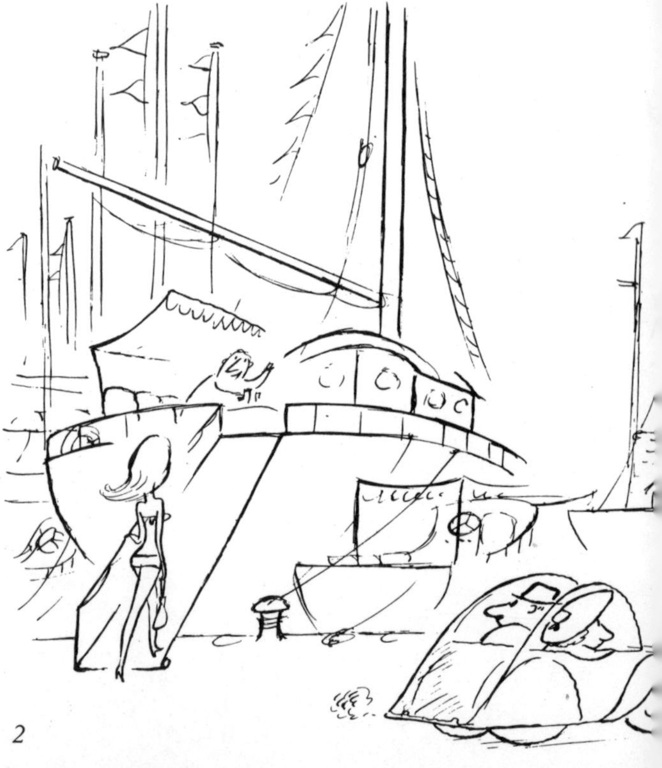

2

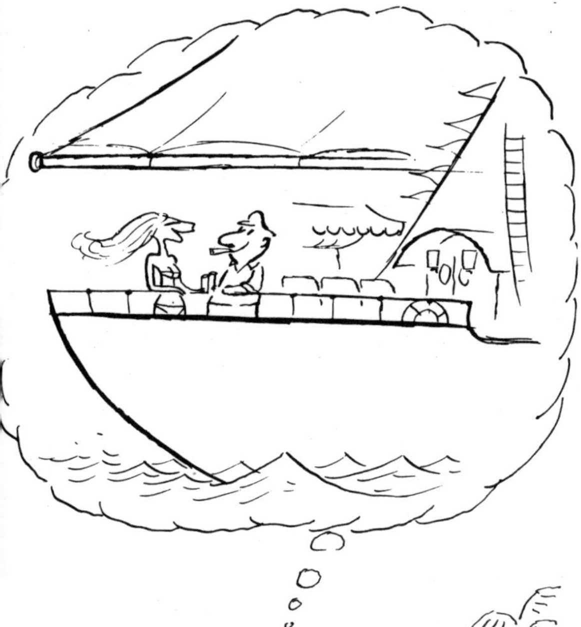

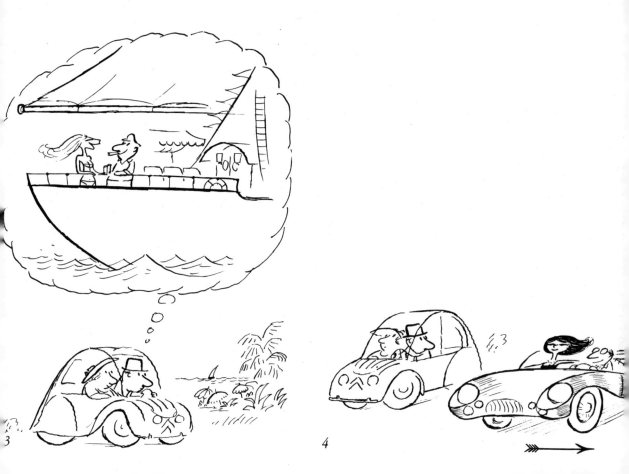

3

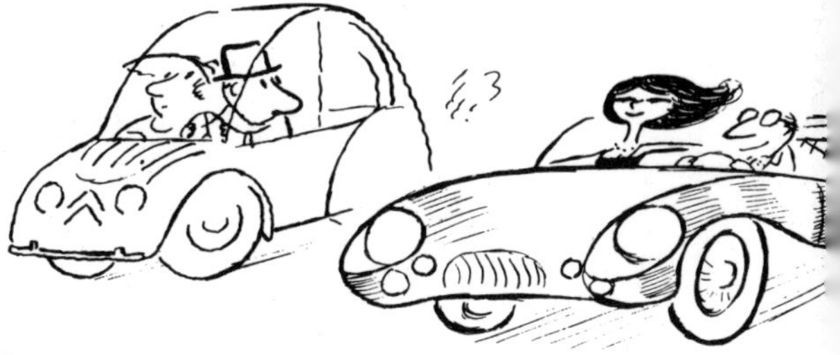

4

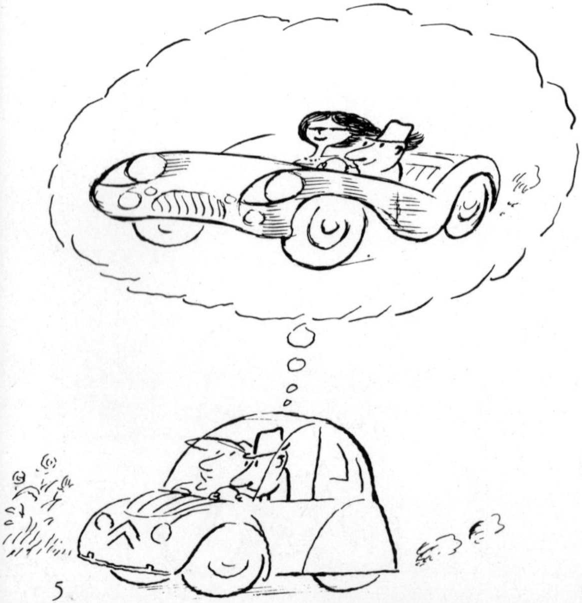

5

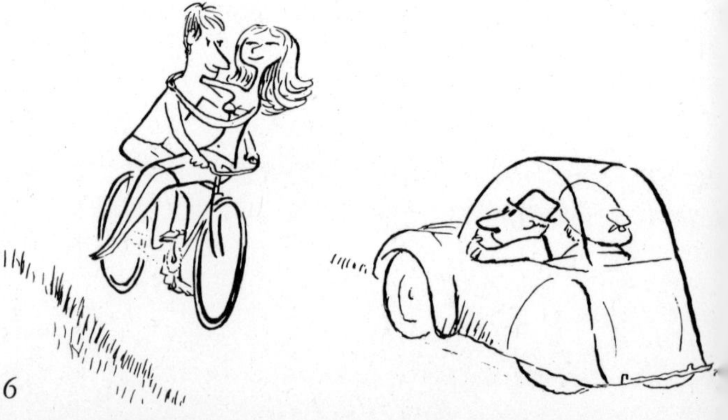

6

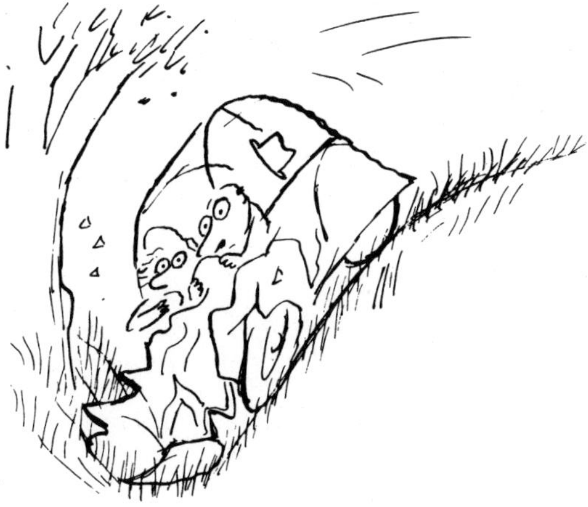

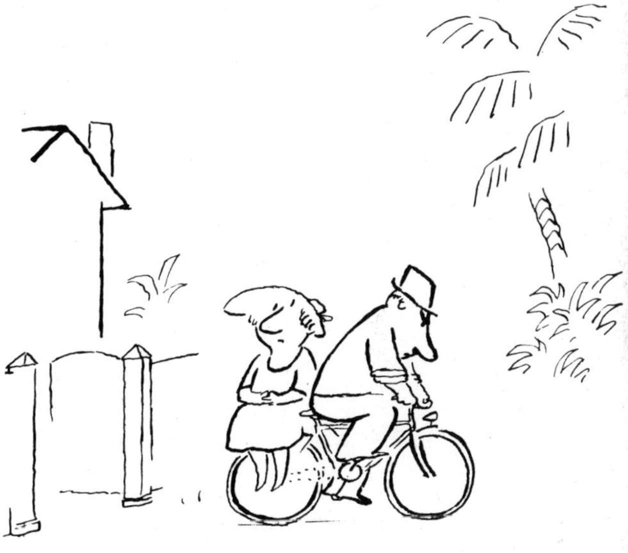

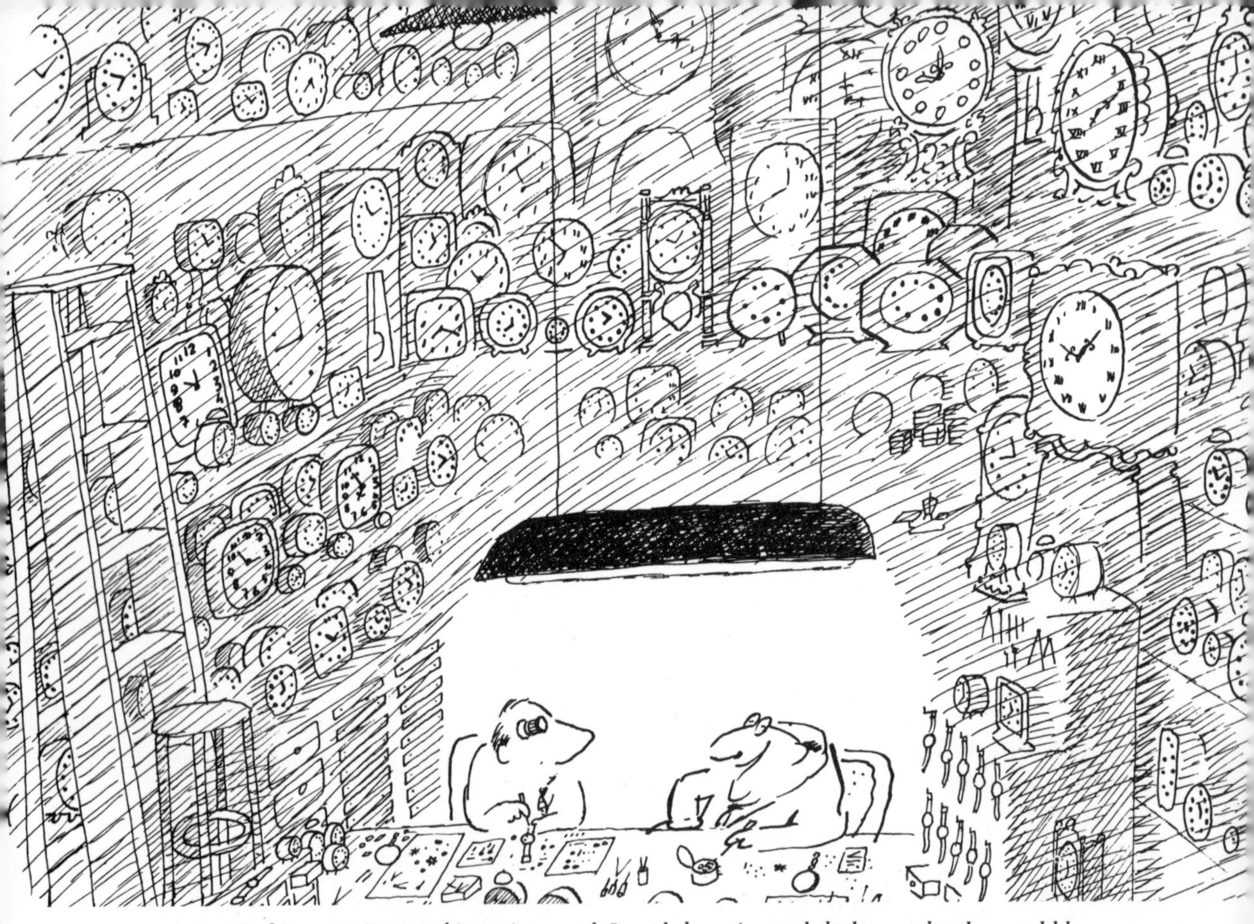

–And in two minutes, thirty-six seconds I made her mine and she knew what love could be.

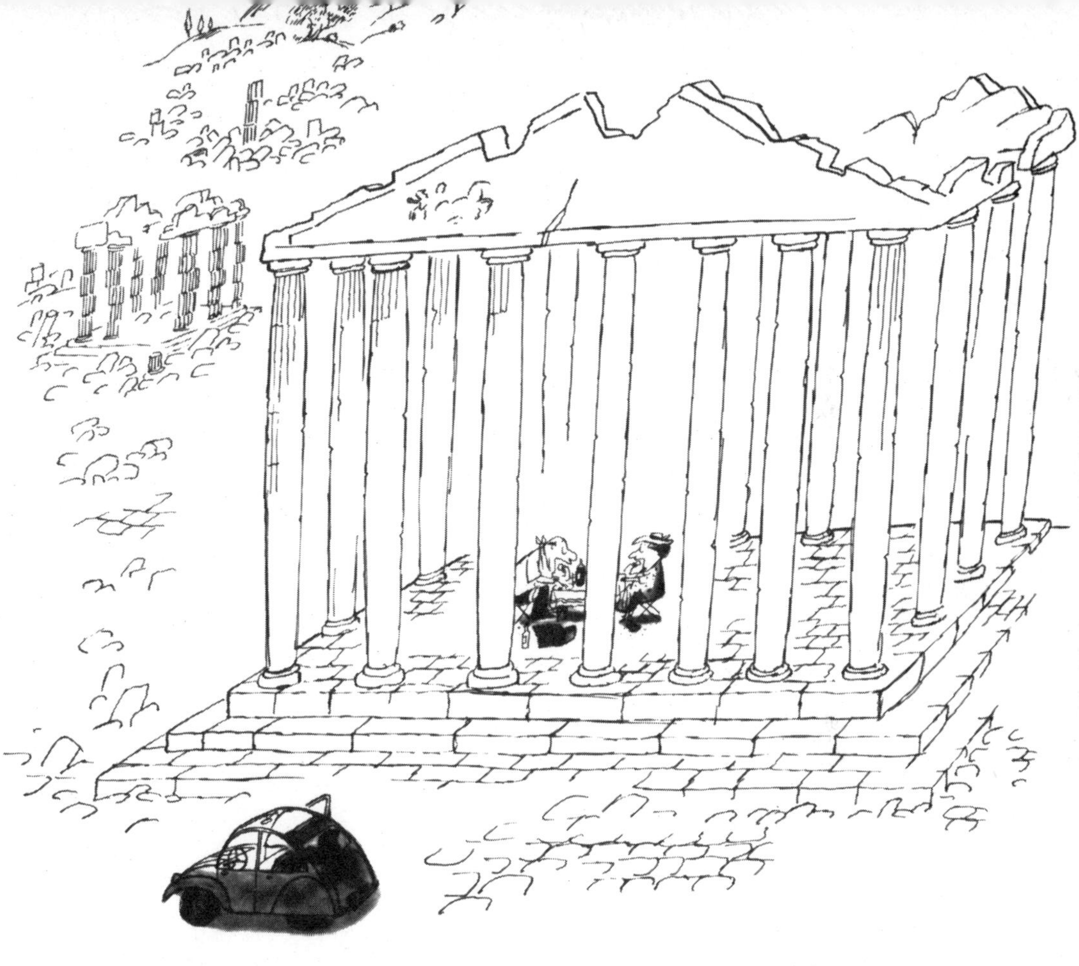

3

4

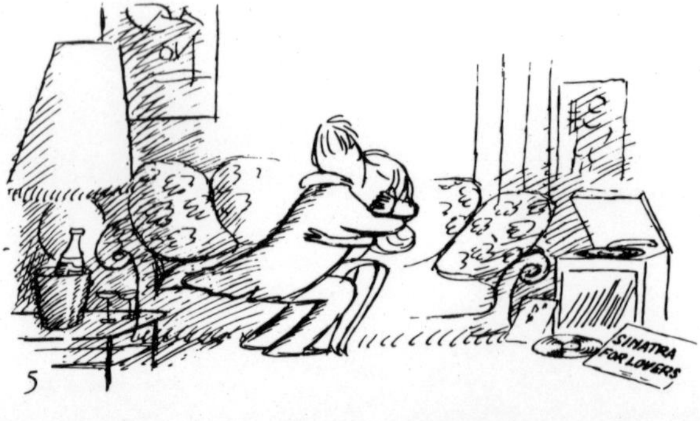
SINATRA
FOR LOVERS

5

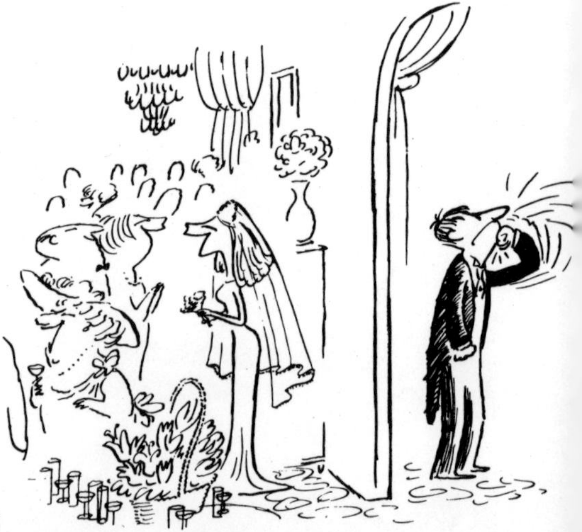

6

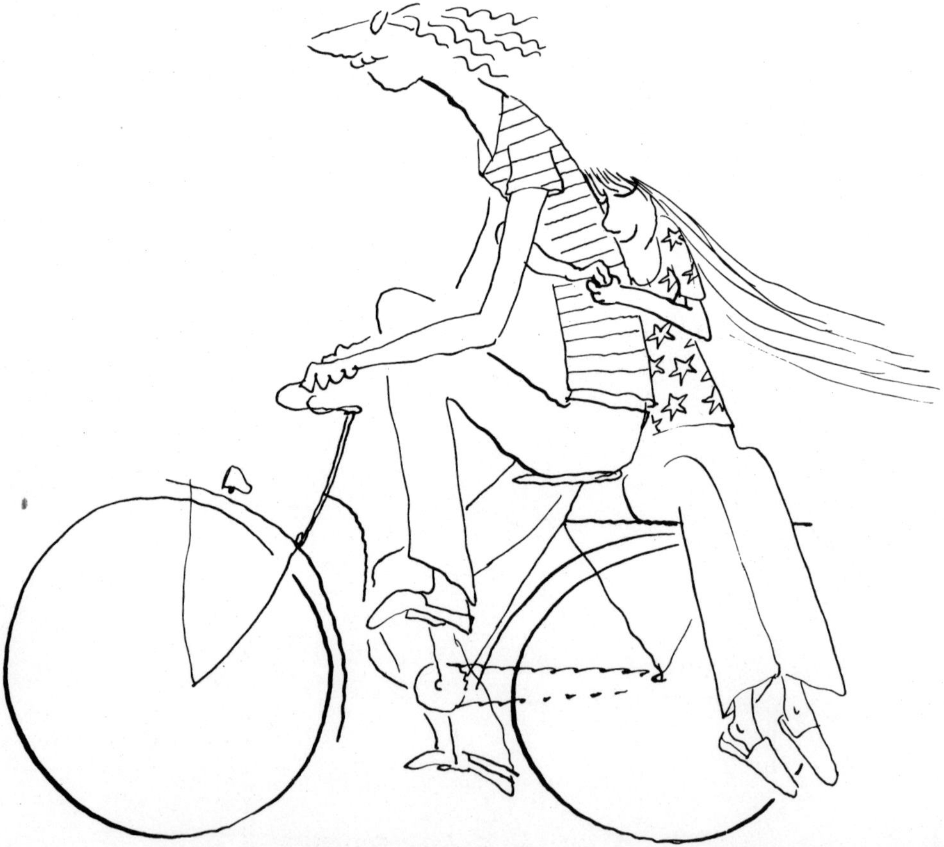

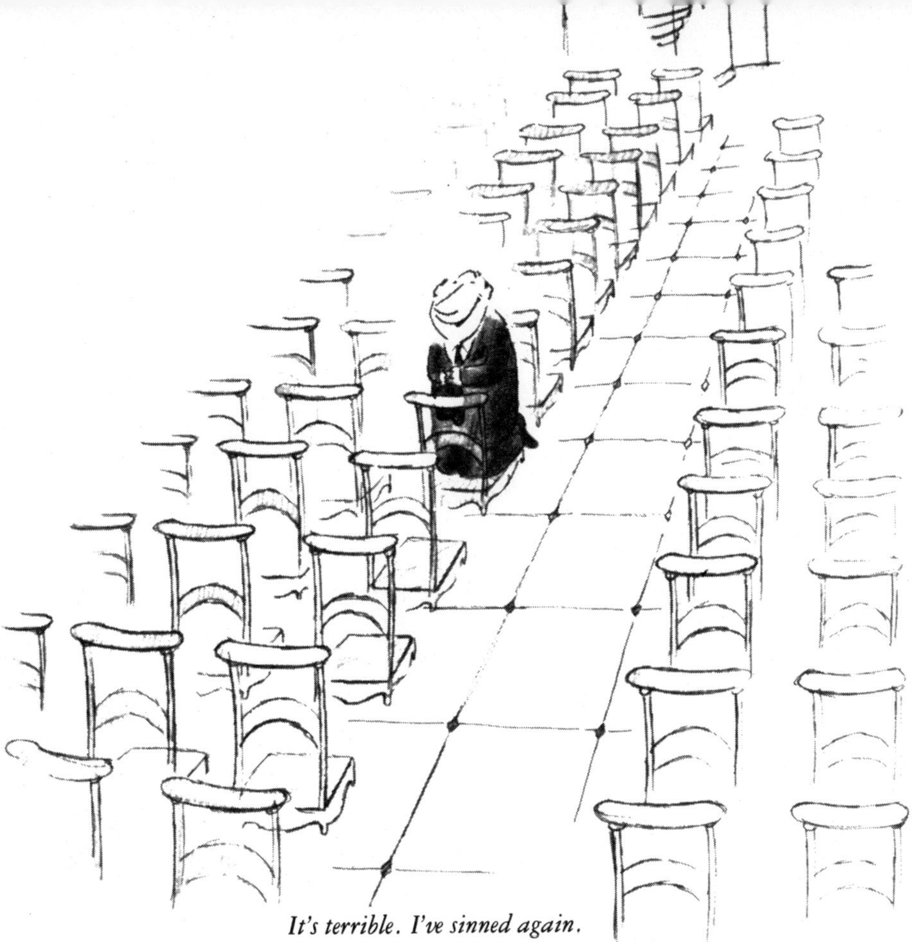

It's terrible. I've sinned again.

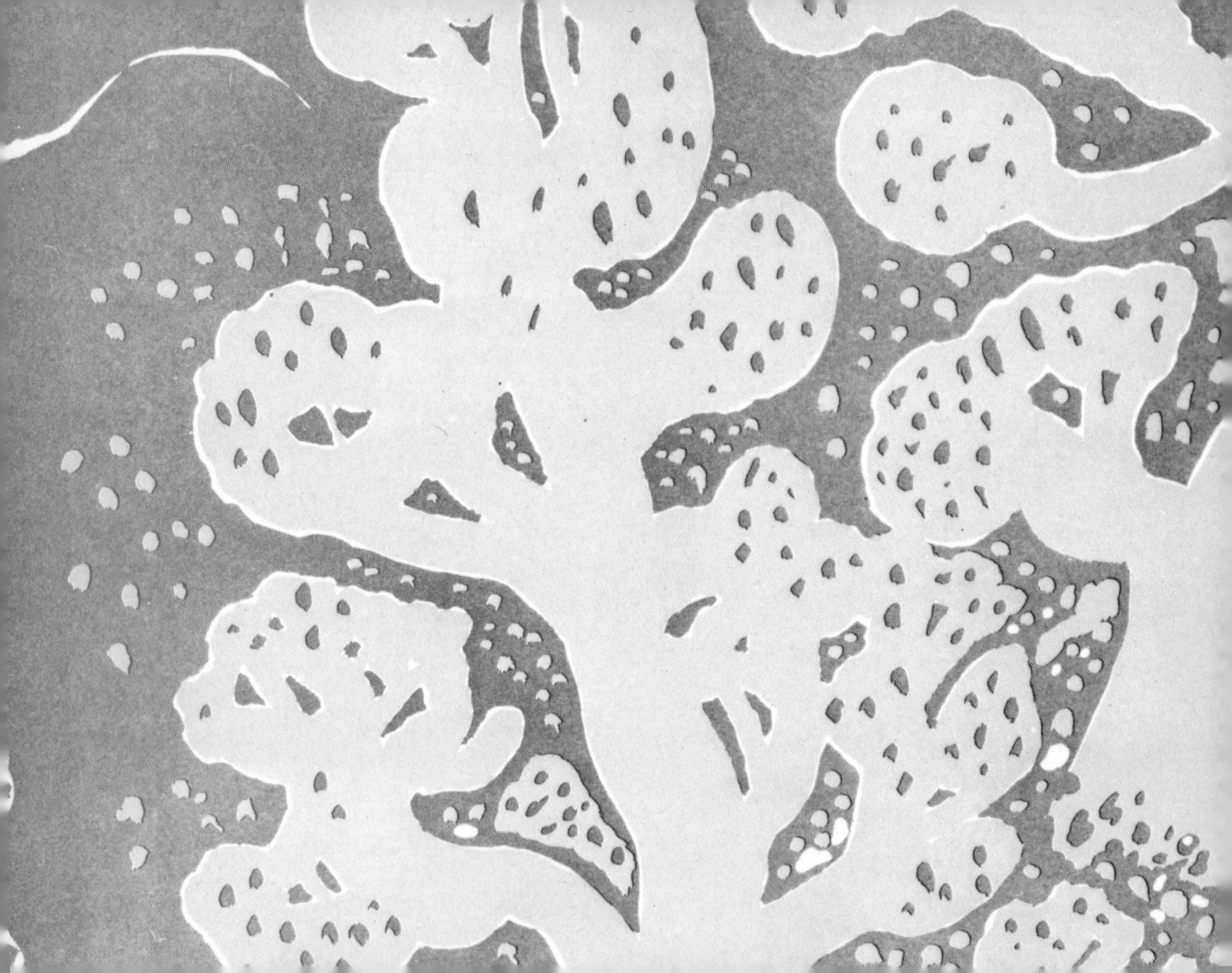

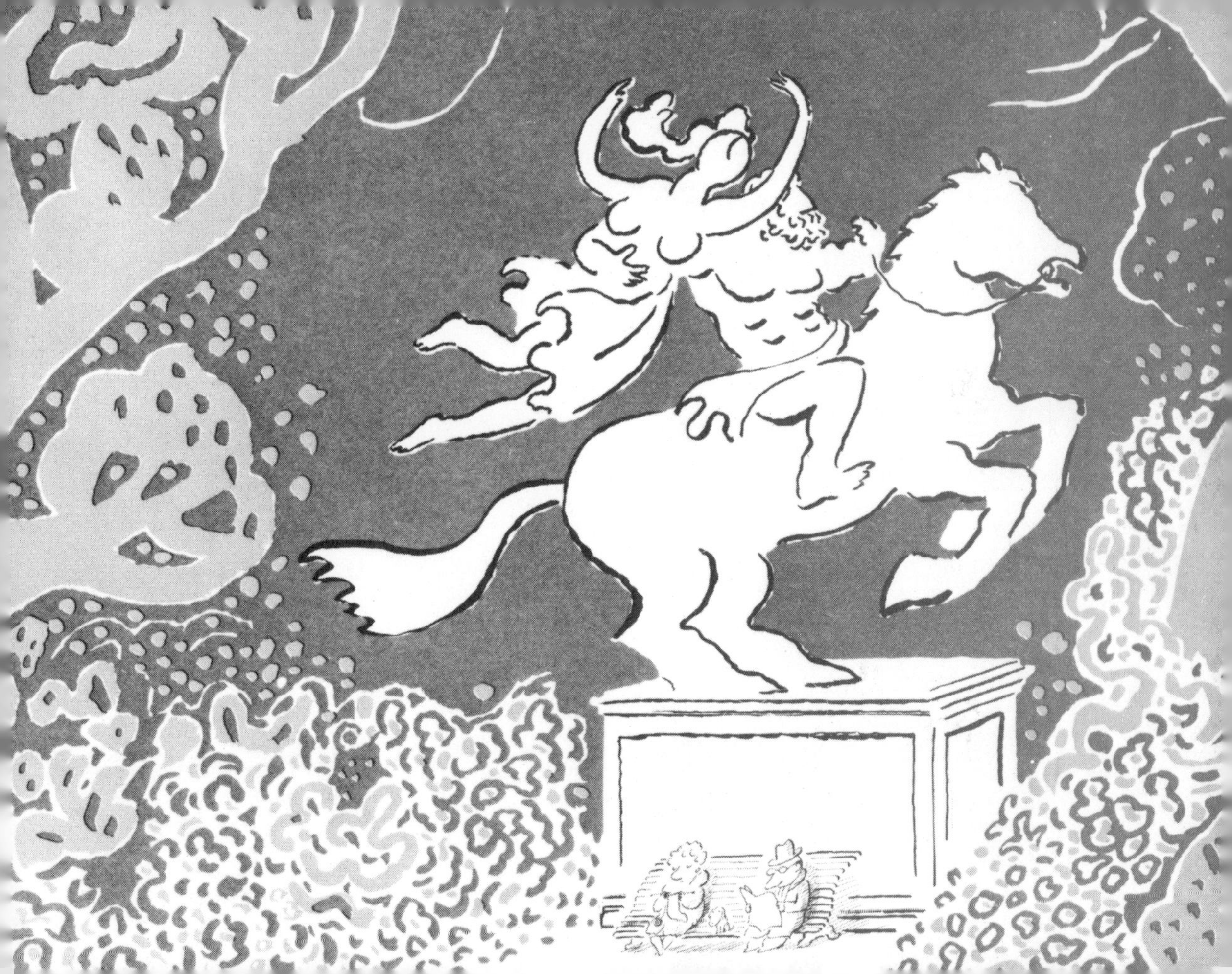

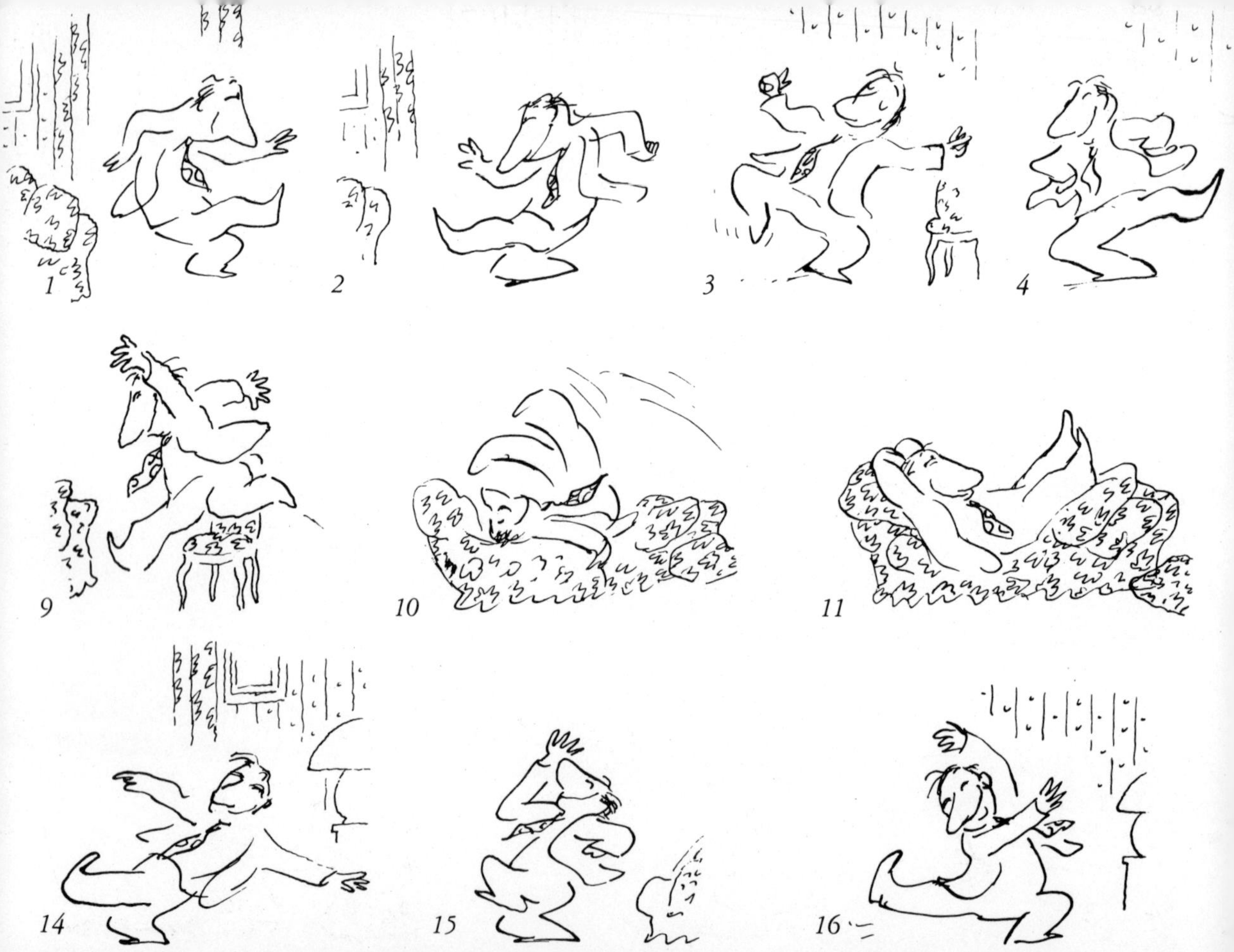
1
2
3
4
9
10
11
14
15
16

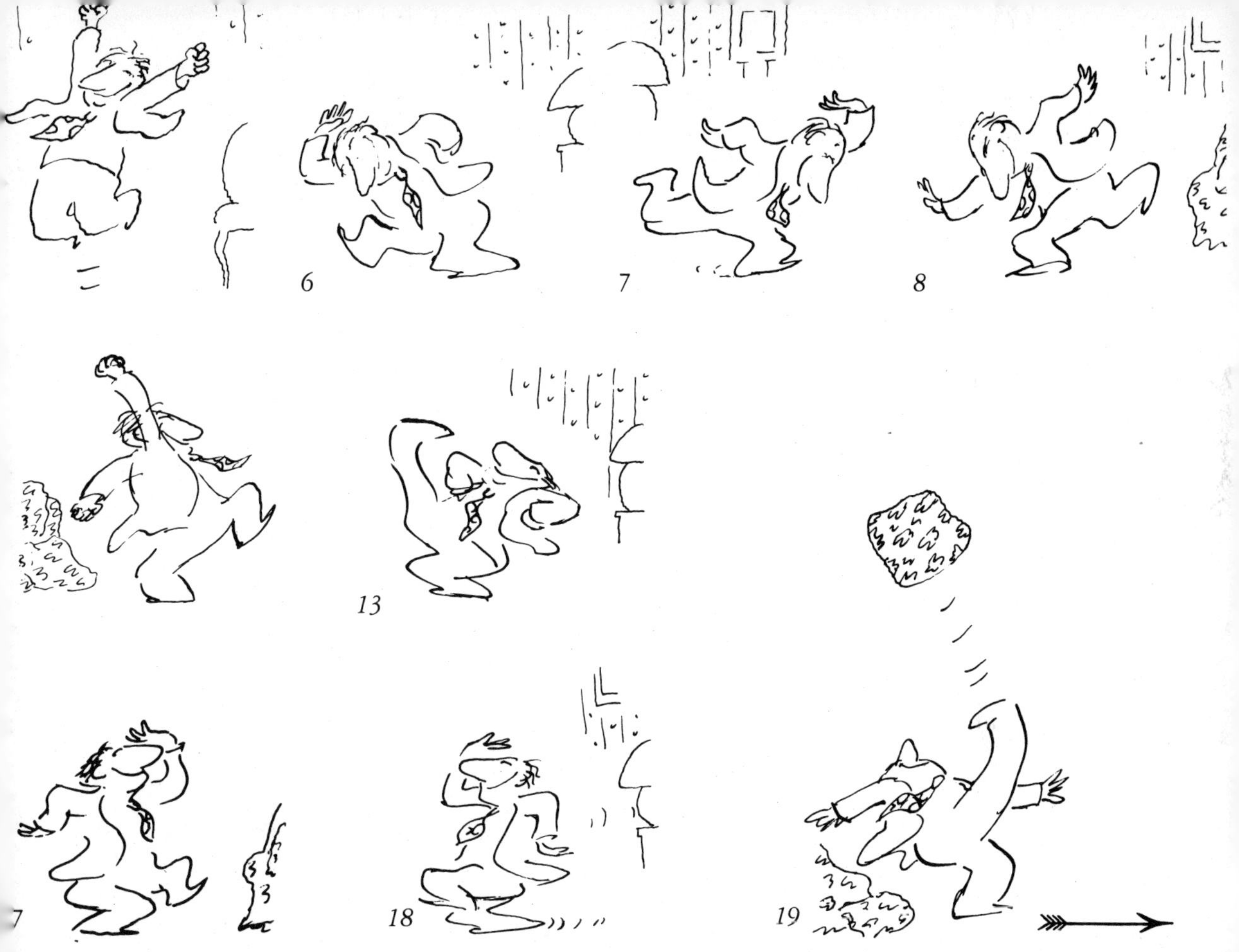
6
7
8
13
7
18
19

I'm in love with another woman.

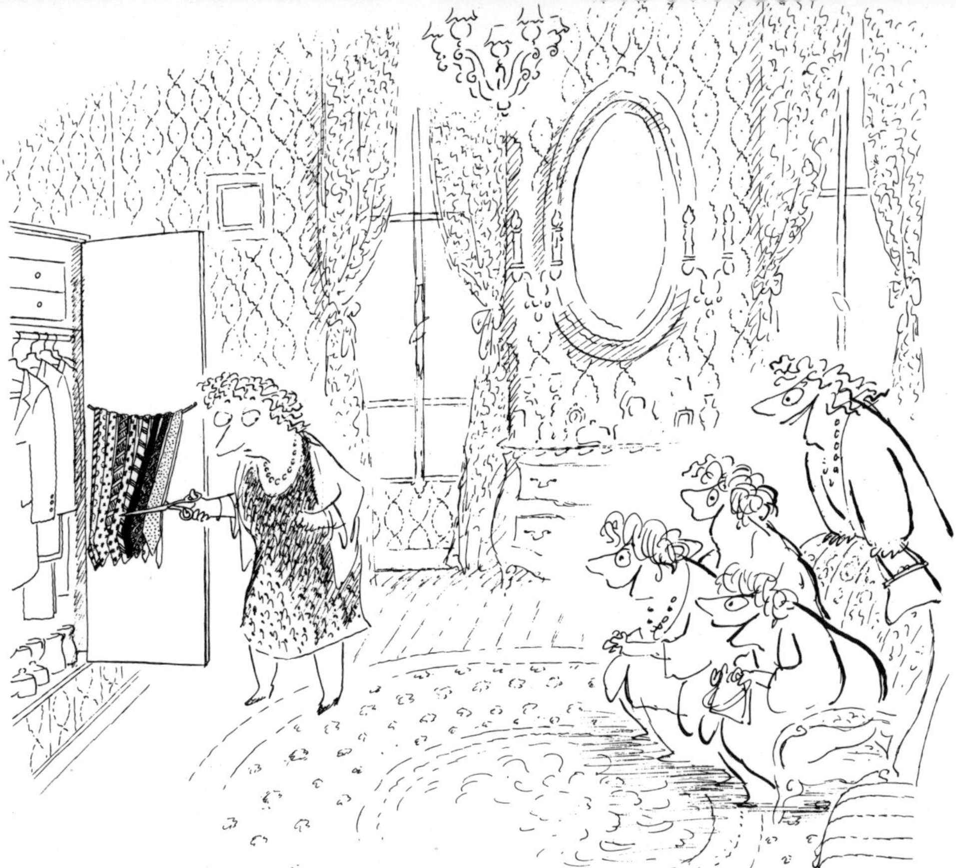

YES!

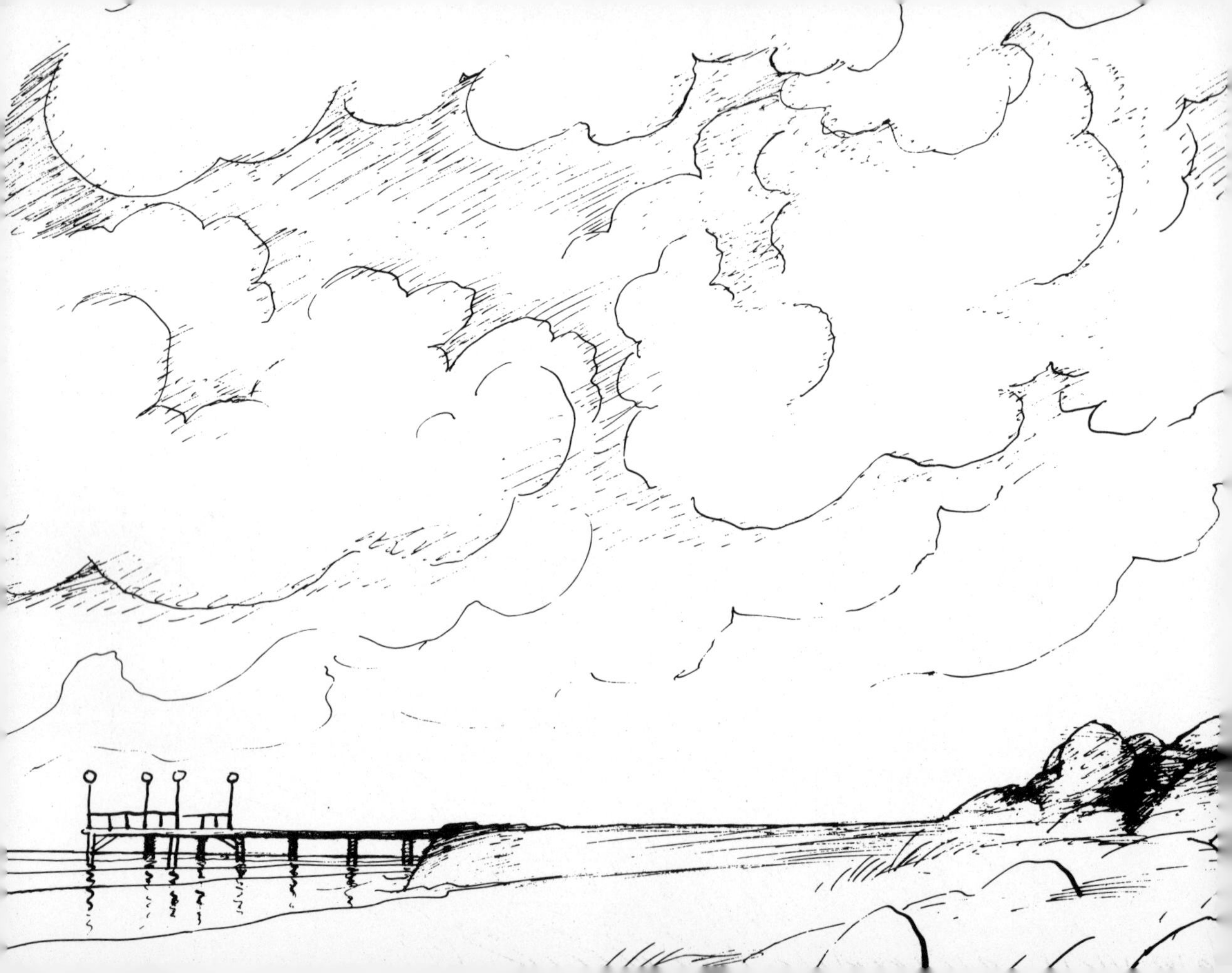

I'm searching for joy. With a J as in Jules.

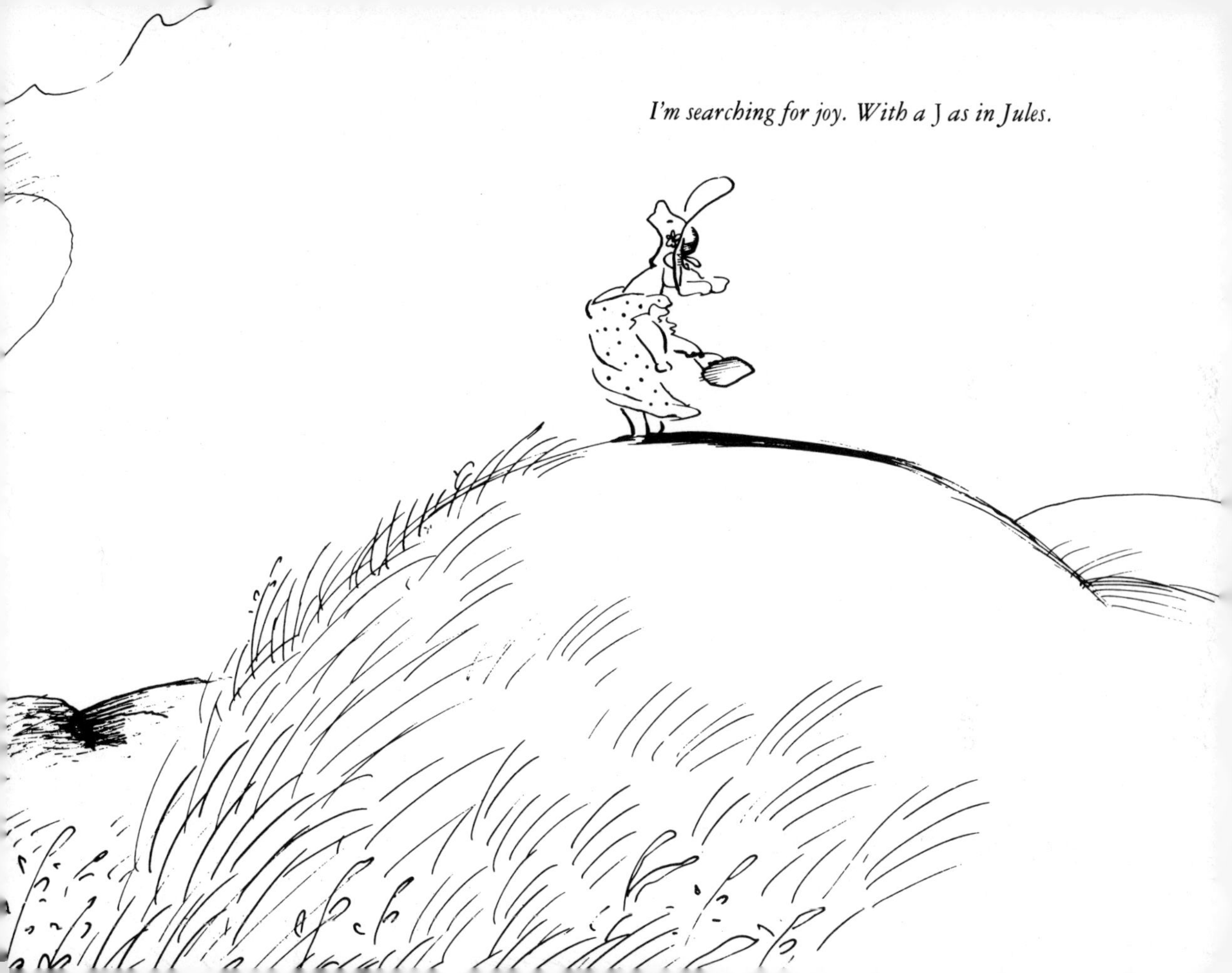

1

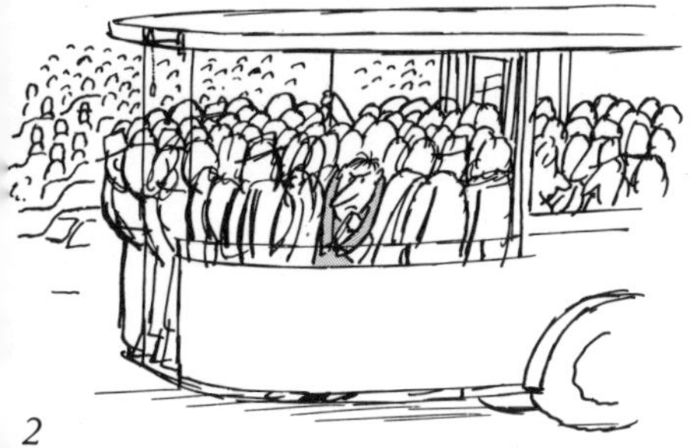

2

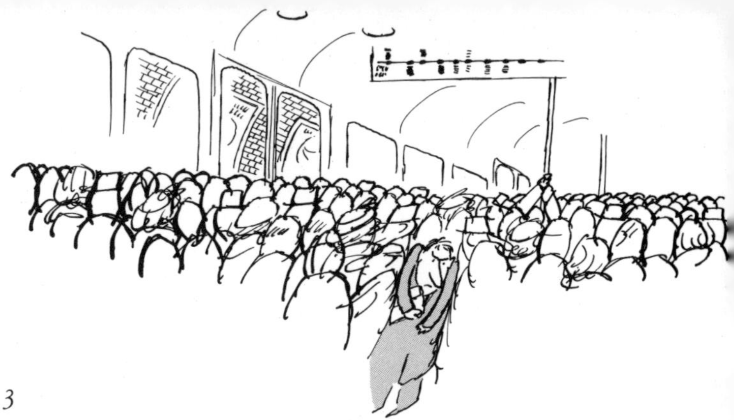

3

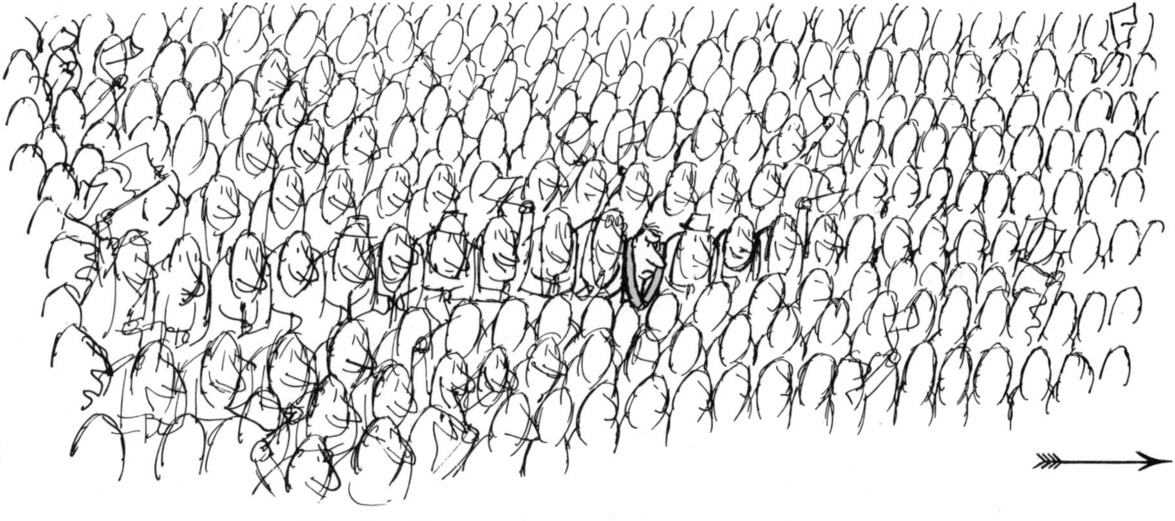

4

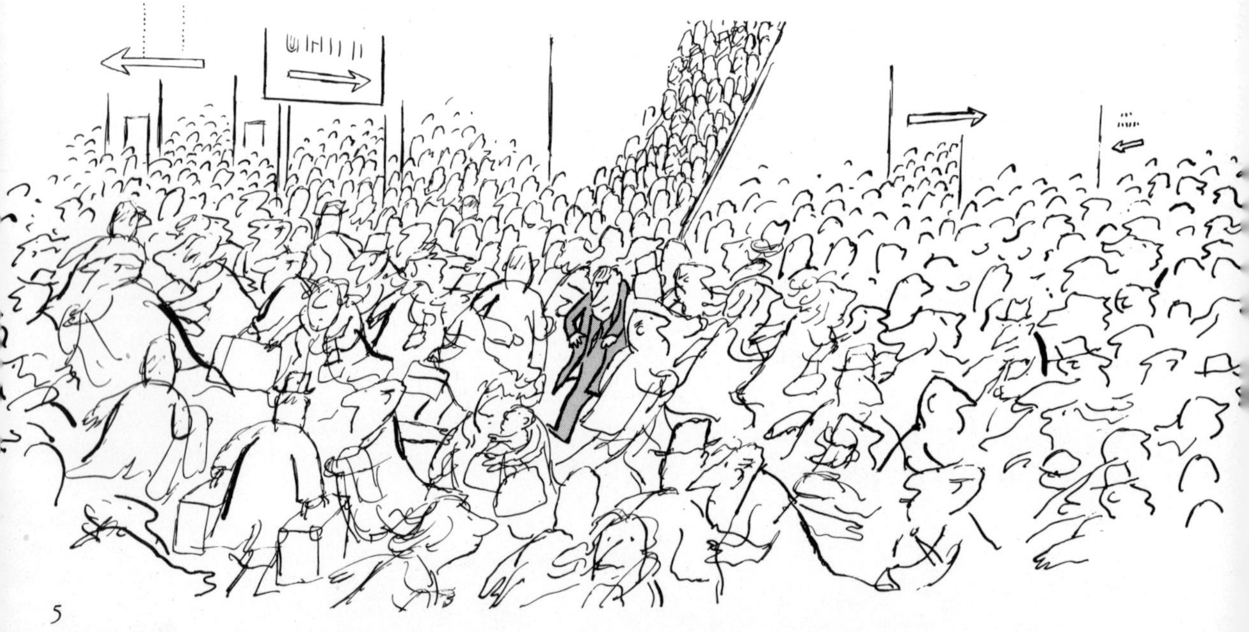

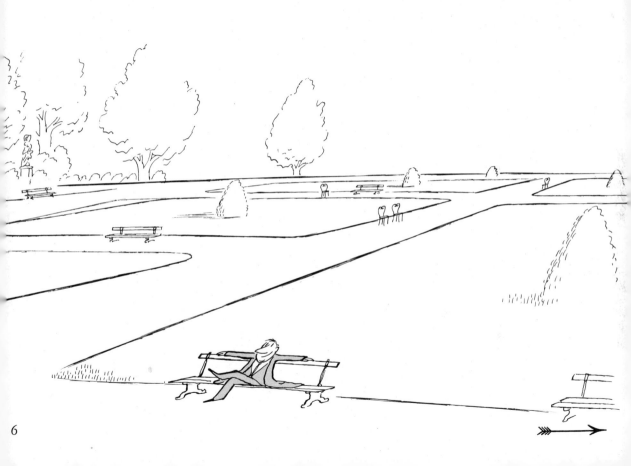

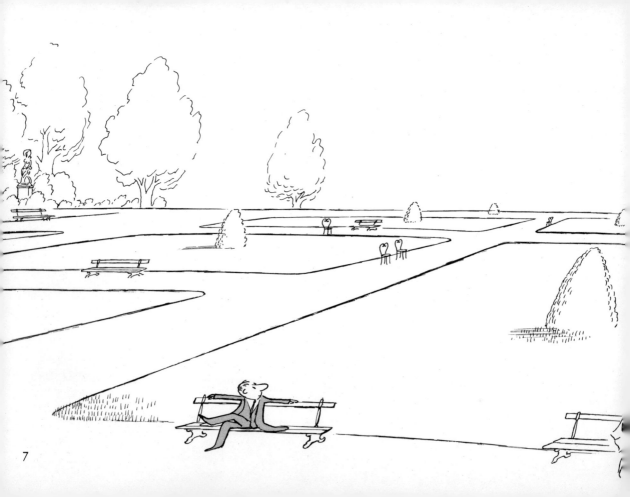

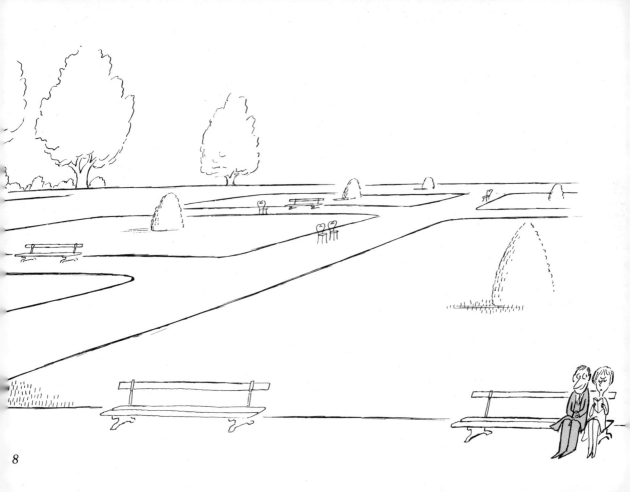

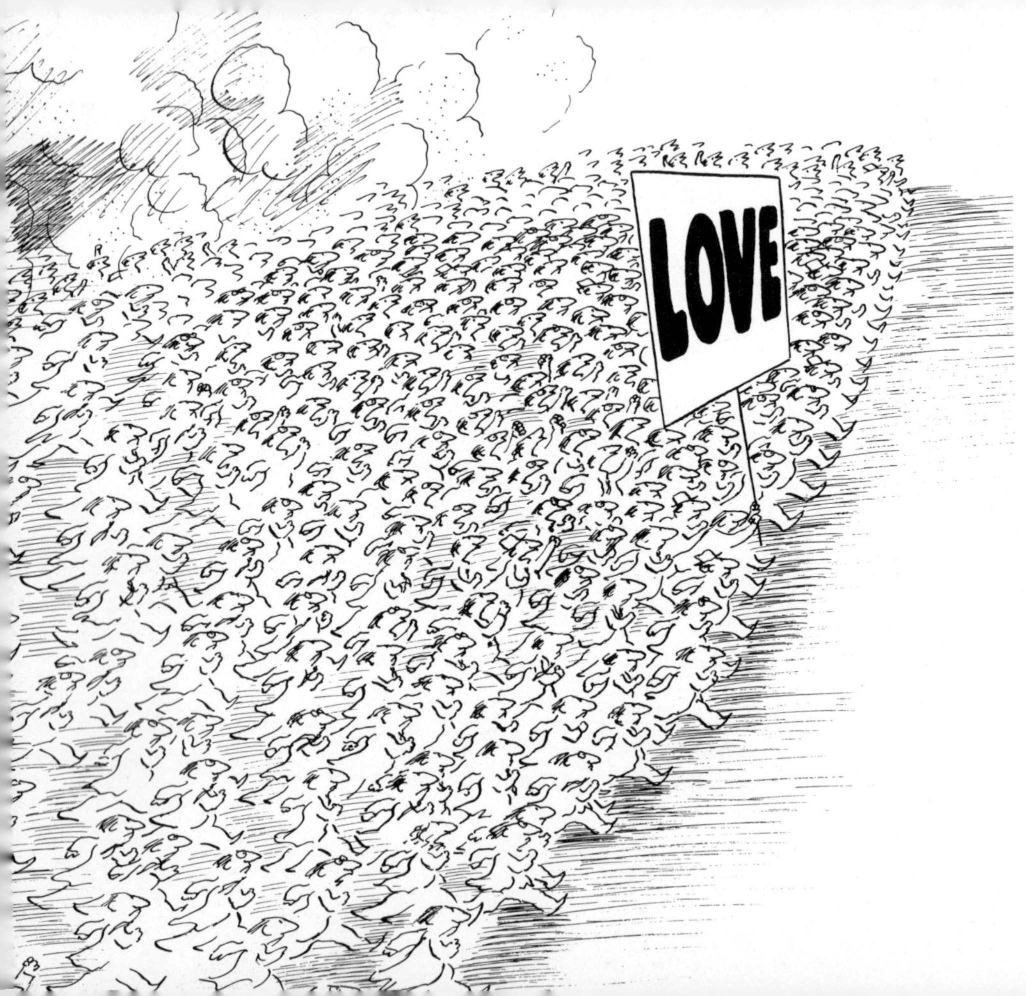
LOVE

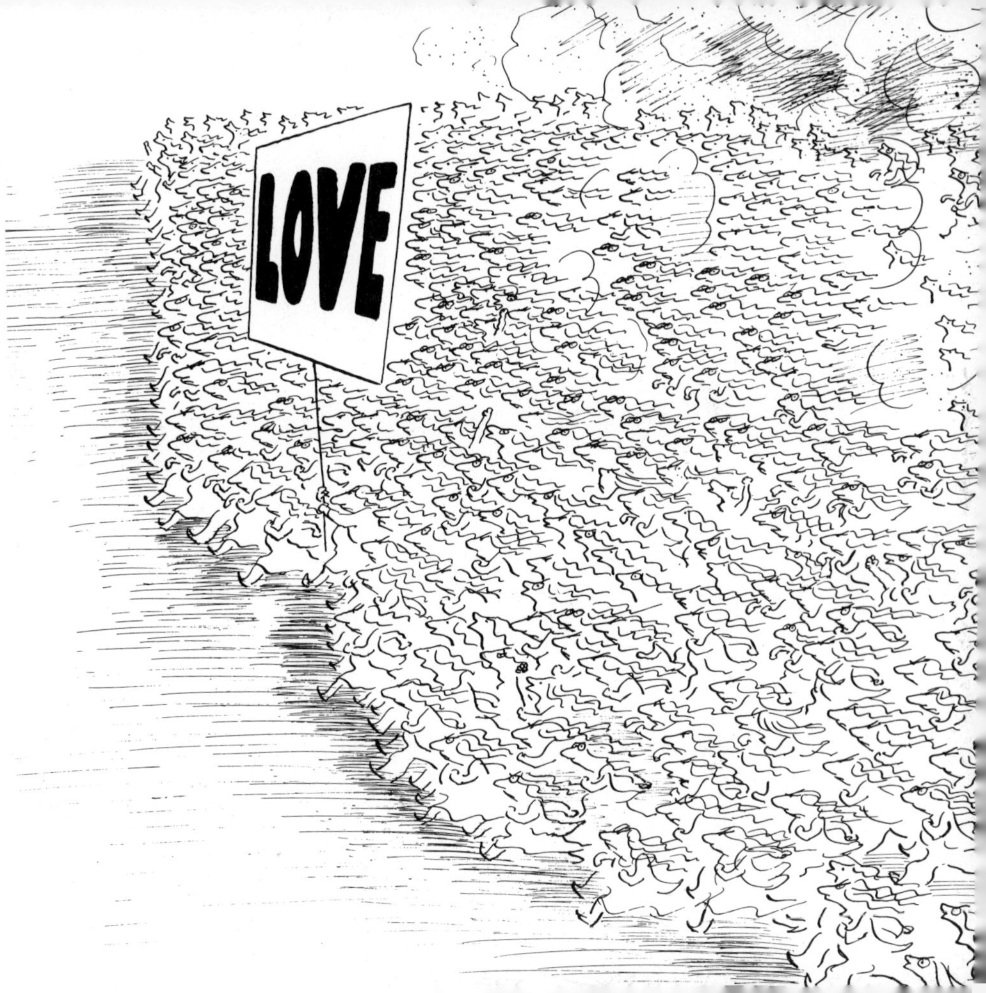
LOVE

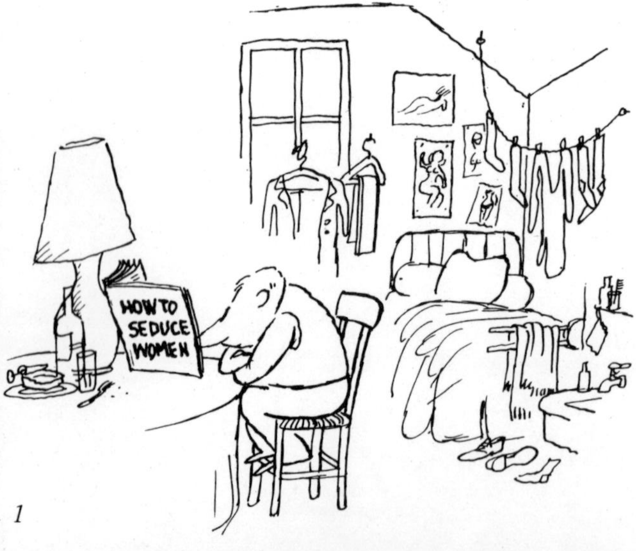
HOW TO
SEDUCE
WOMEN

1

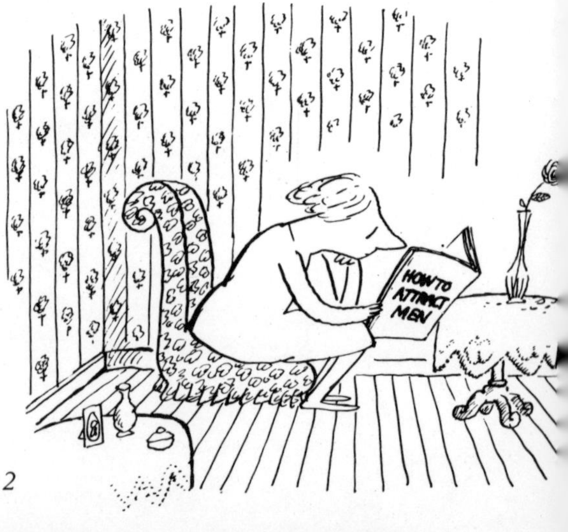
HOW TO
ATTRACT
MEN

2

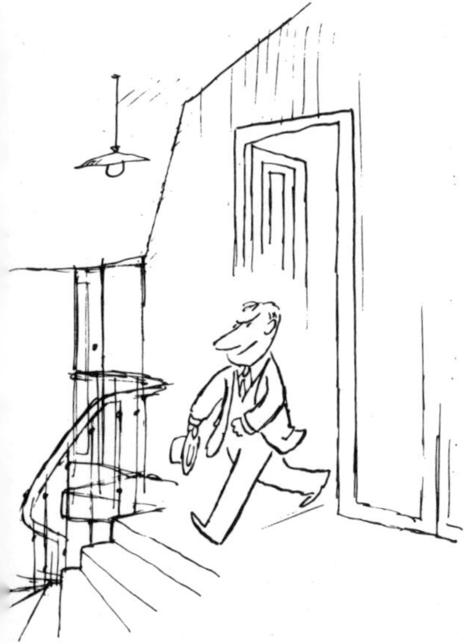

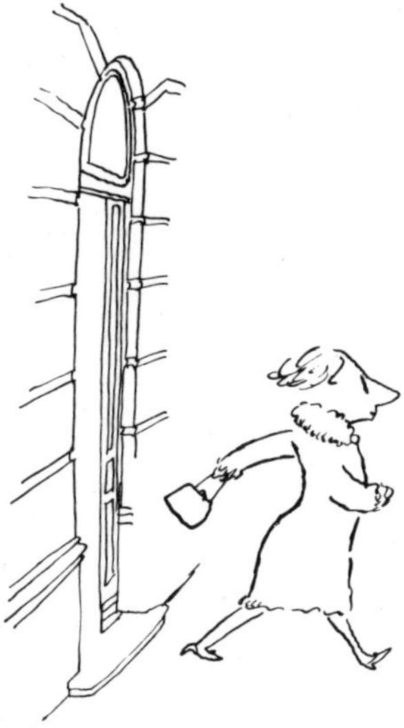

4

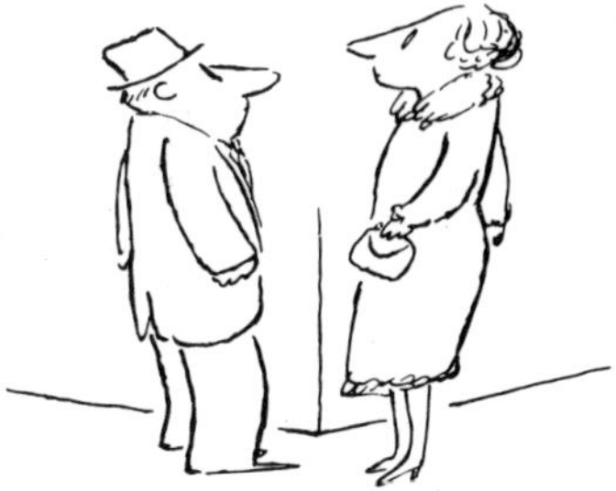

5

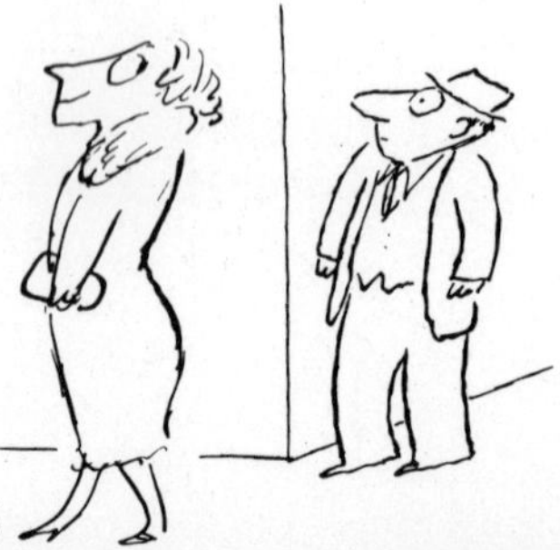

6

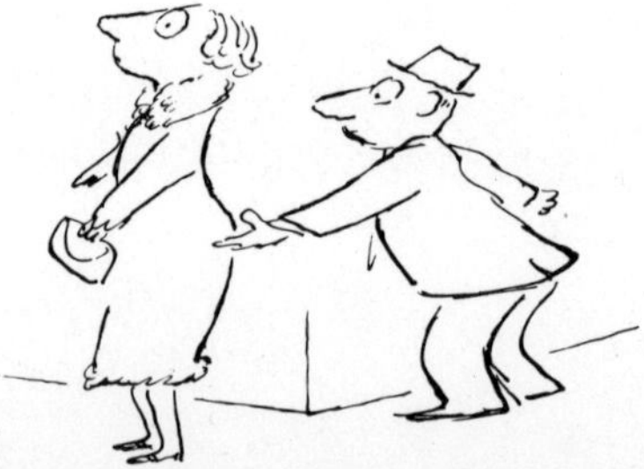

7

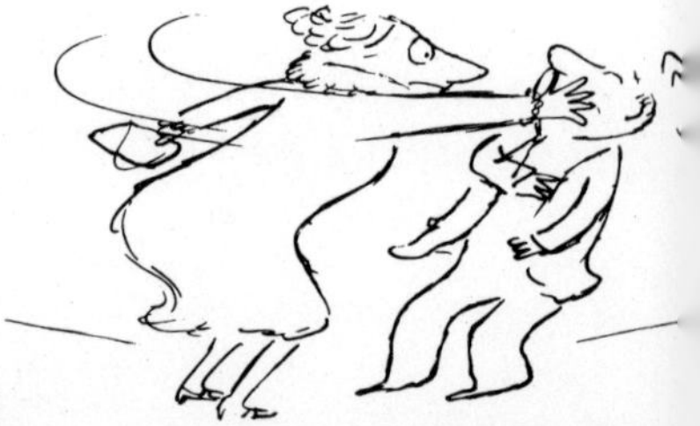

8

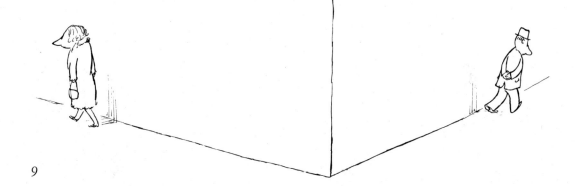

9

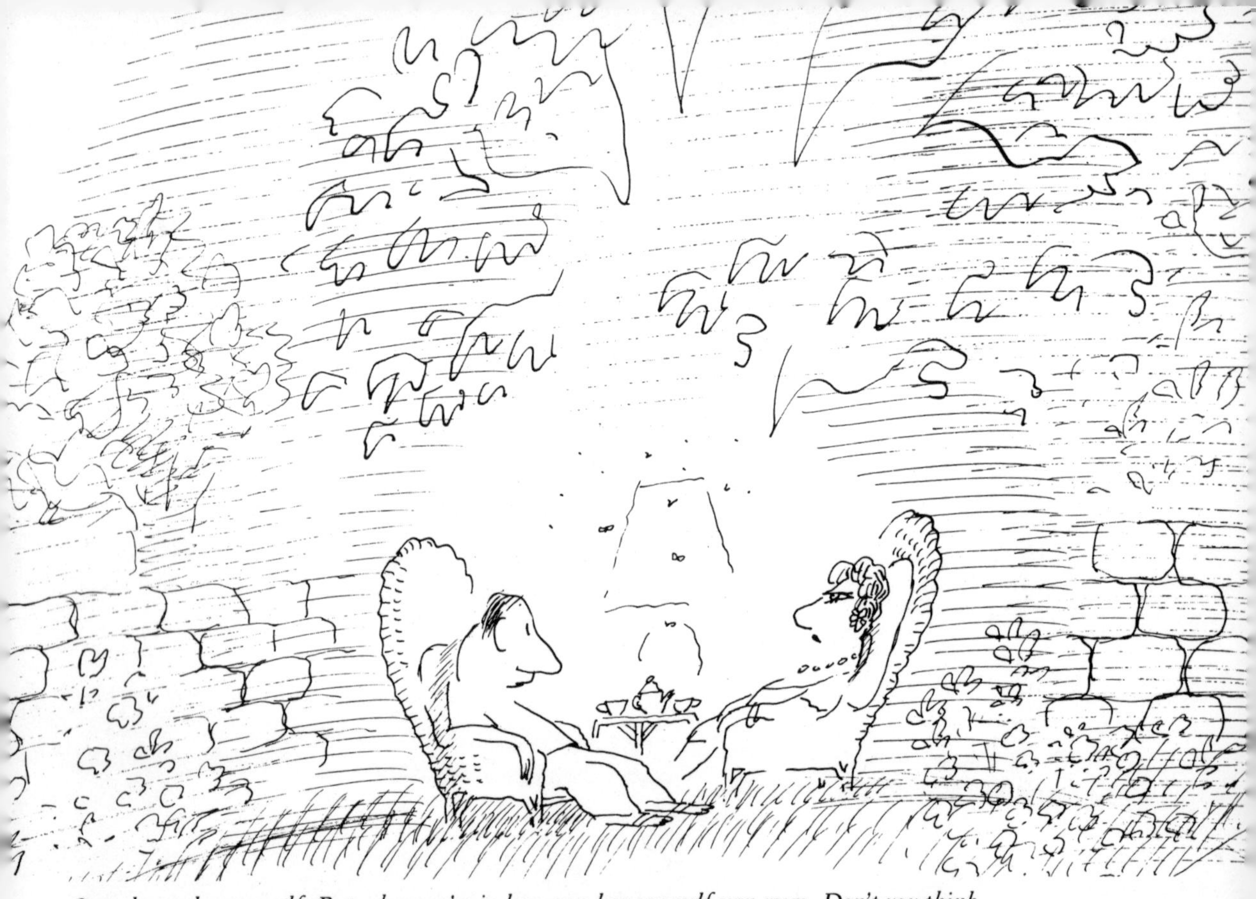

One always loves oneself. But when you're in love, you love yourself even more. Don't you think that was asking too much of us?

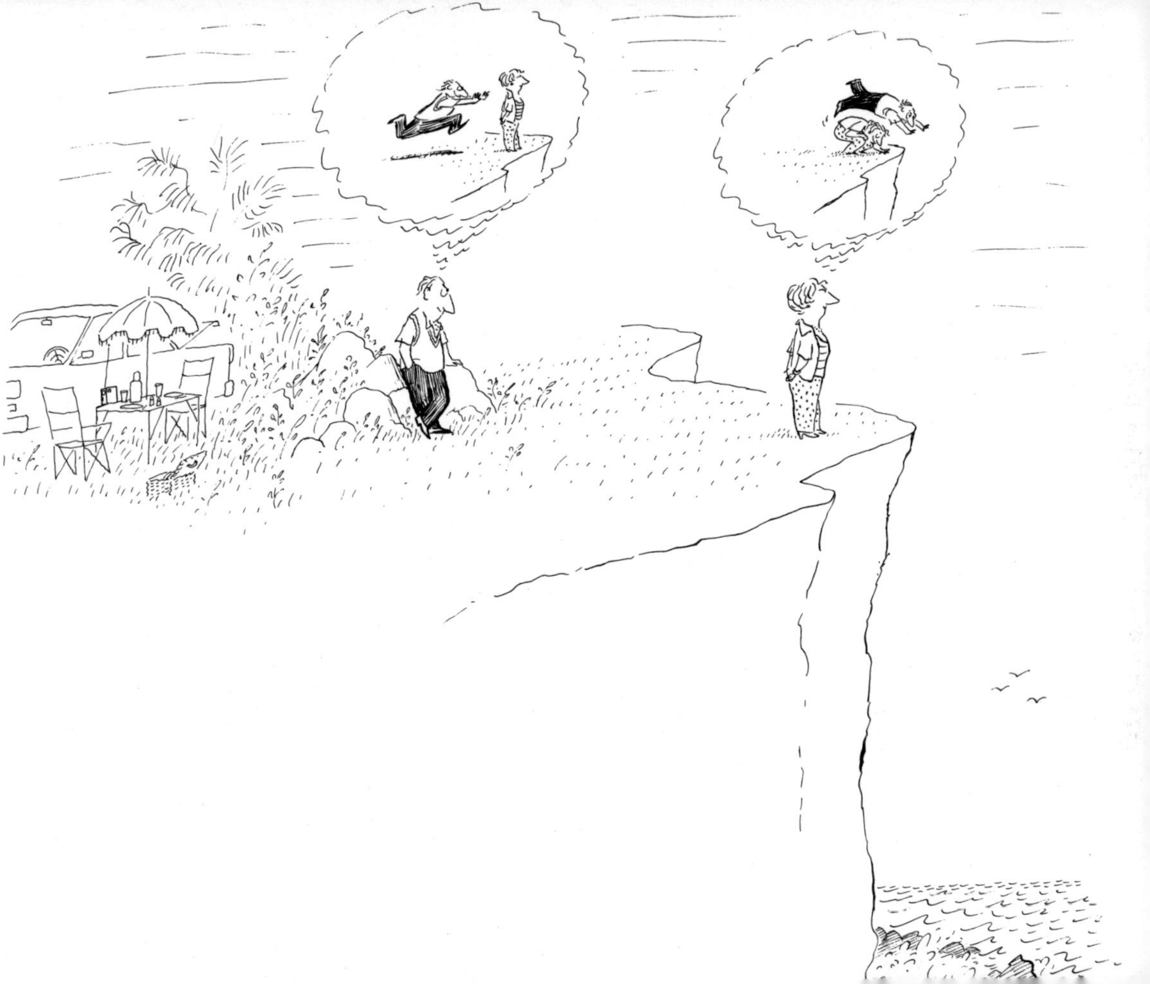

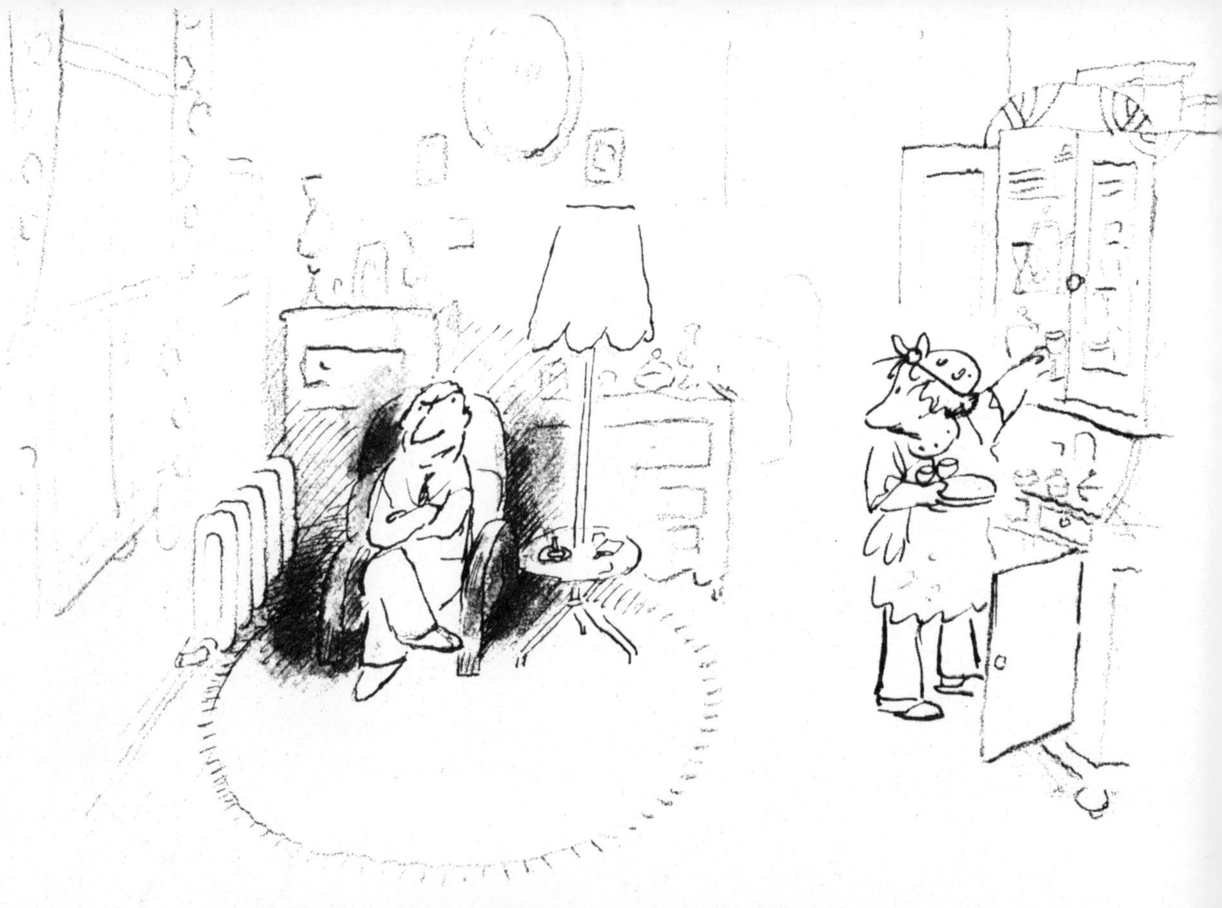

There's going to be serious trouble here when I start exploiting my potential for happiness.

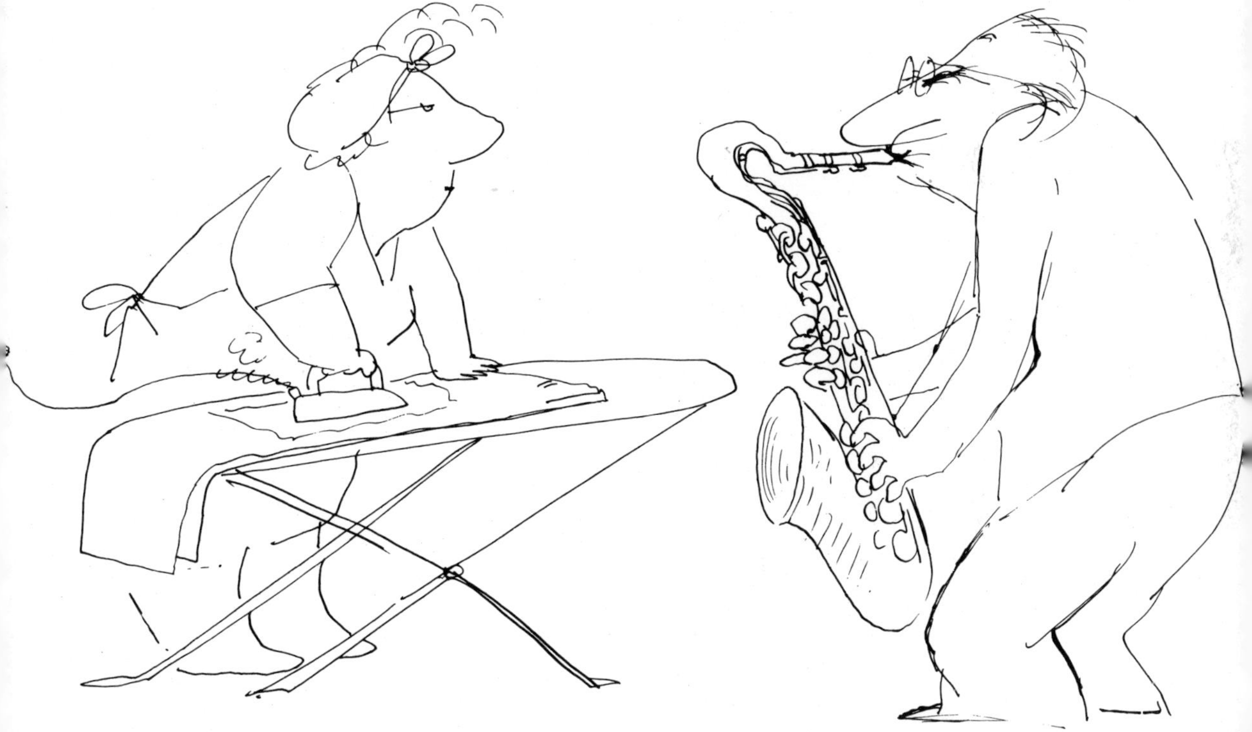

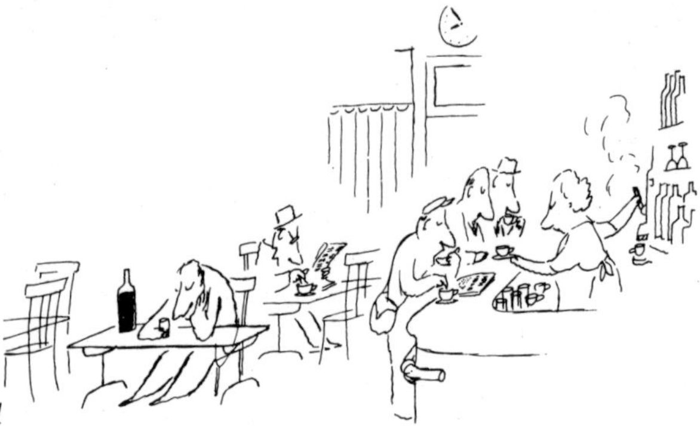
1

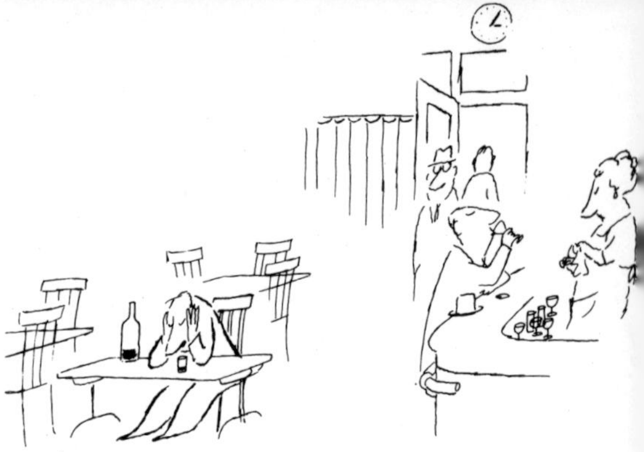
2

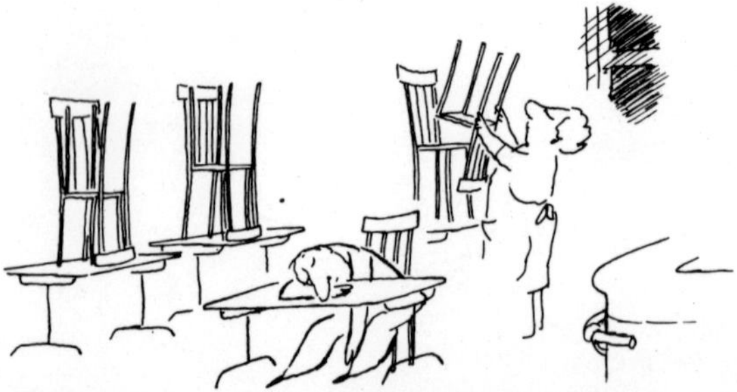
5

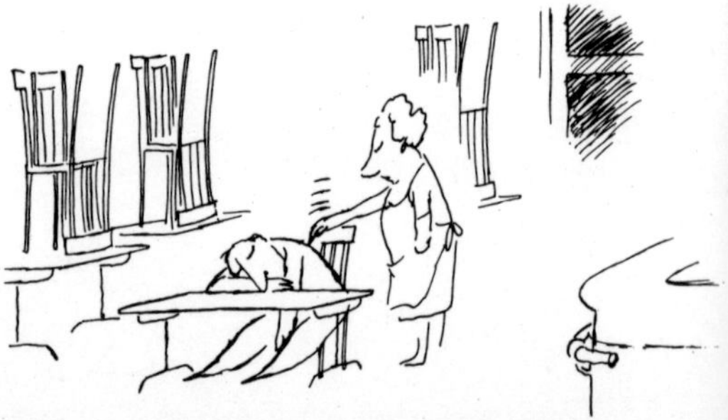
6

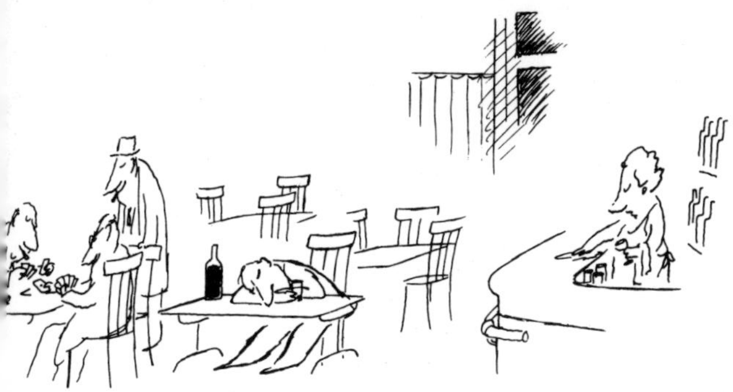

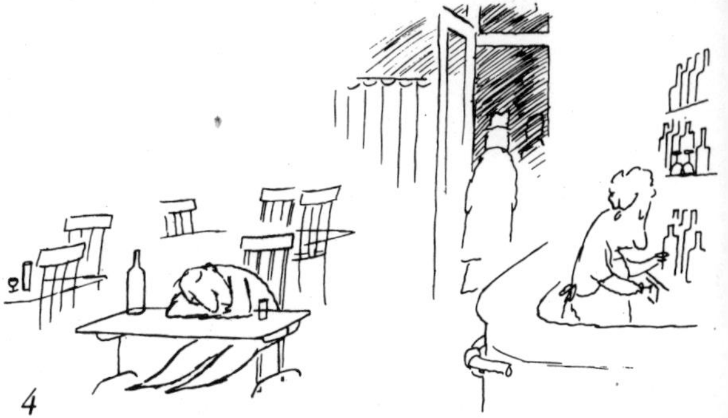

4

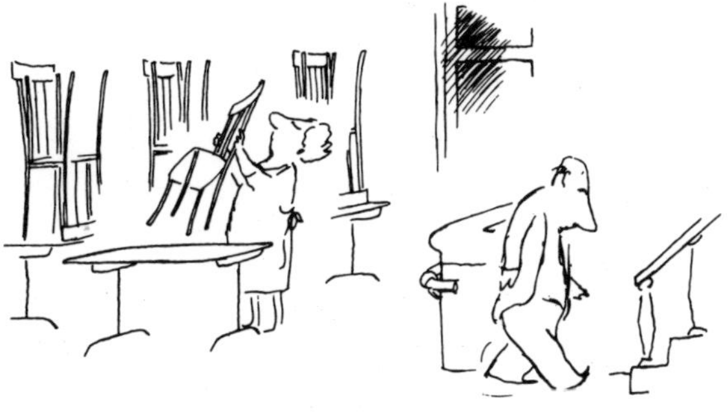

7

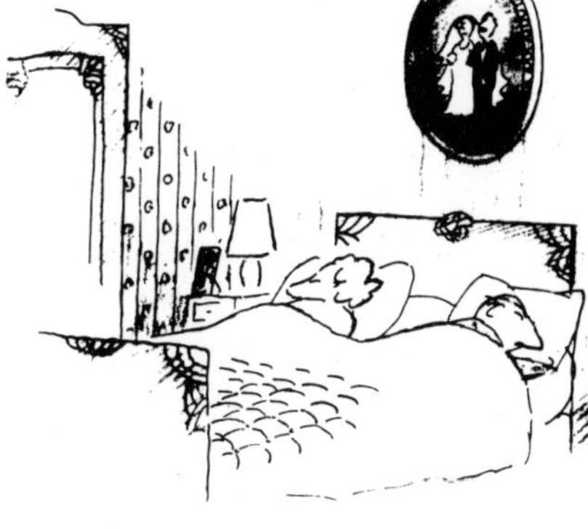

8

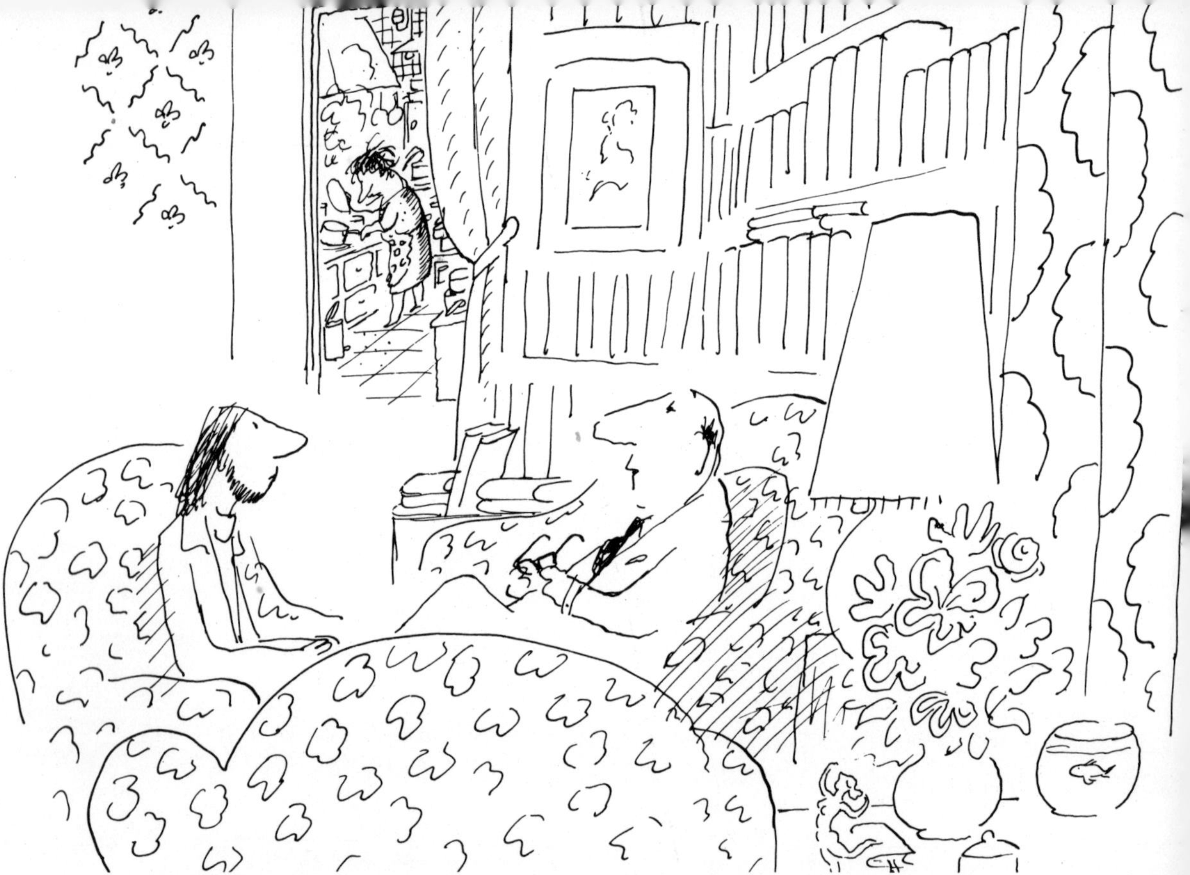

It's a big step in life to understand that the important thing is not only to be loved, but to love. I, for example, love veal stew.

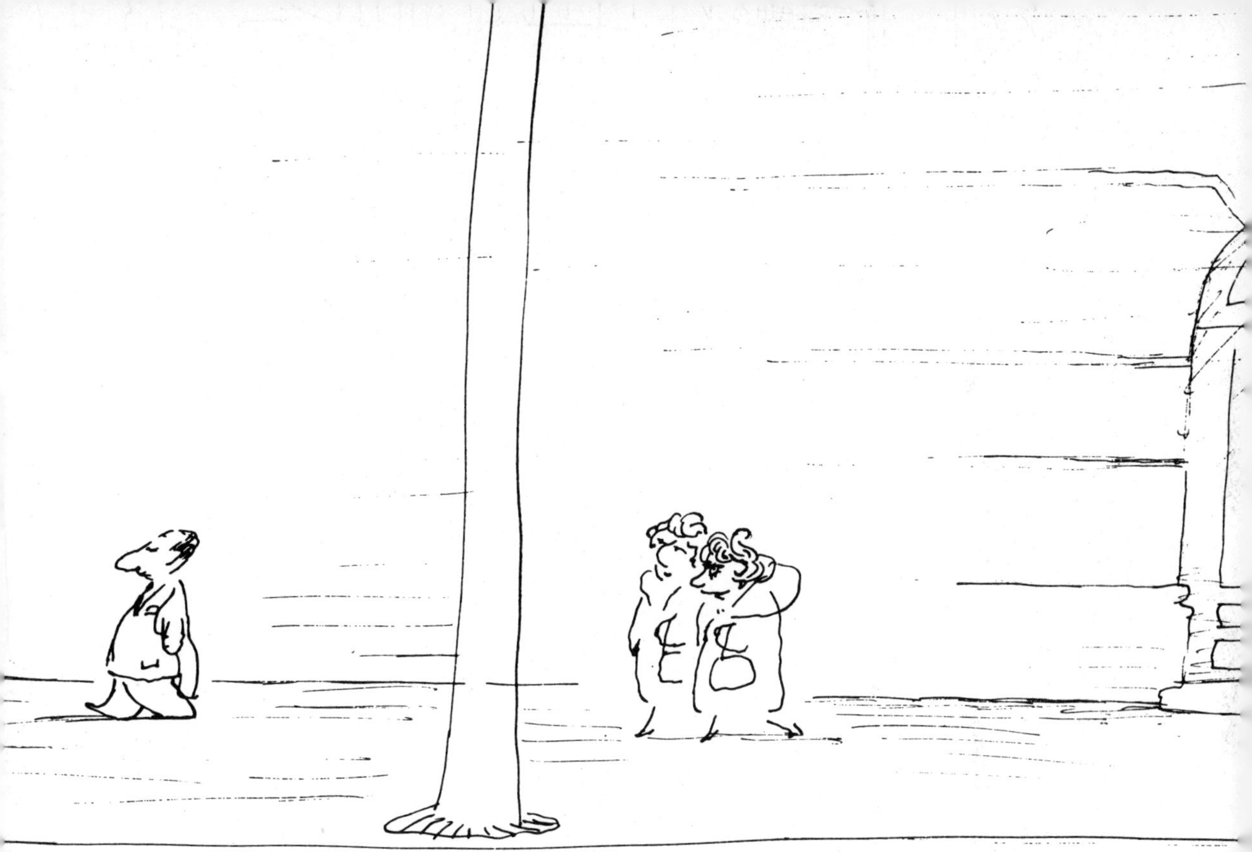

When he compares himself to God, that's perfectly all right; but when he thinks he's the devil, then I really have to laugh.

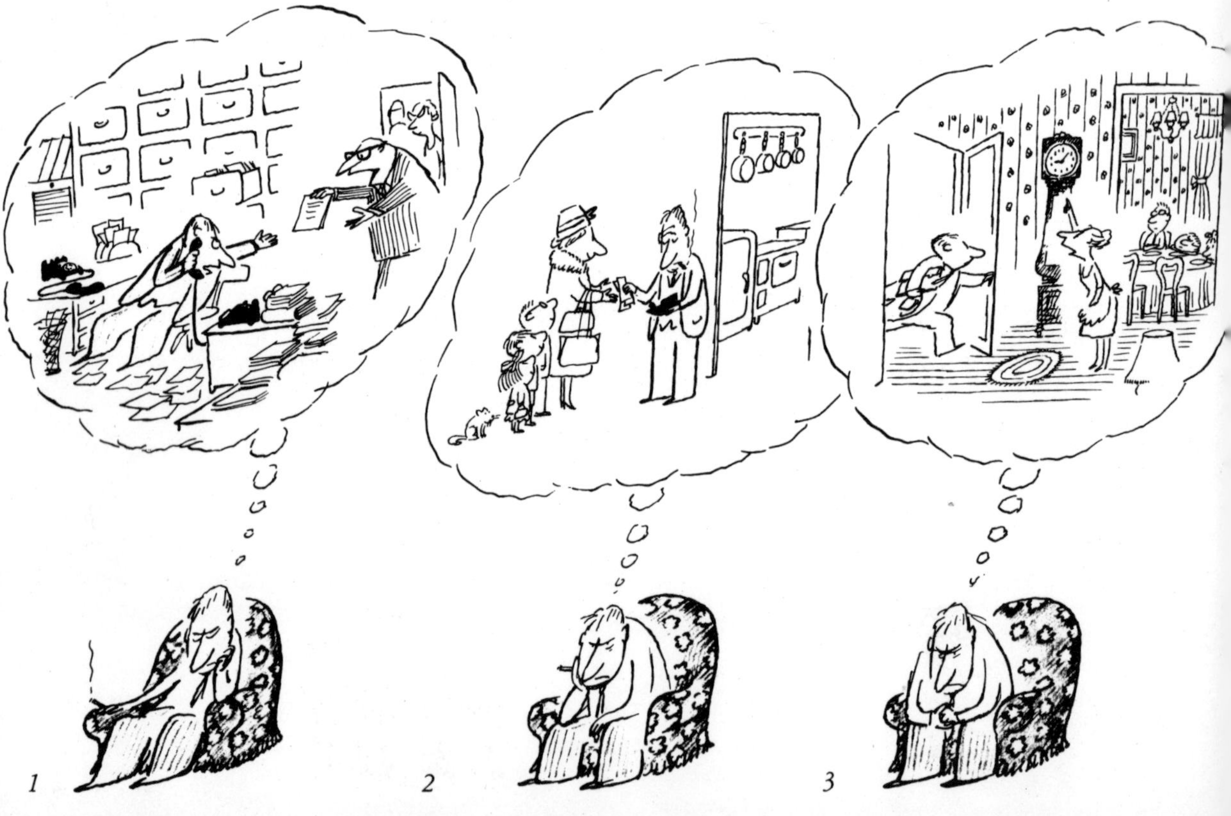
1
2
3

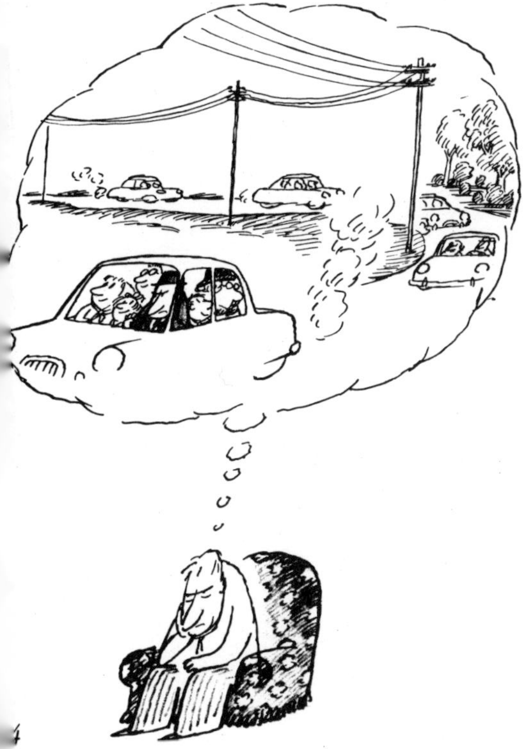

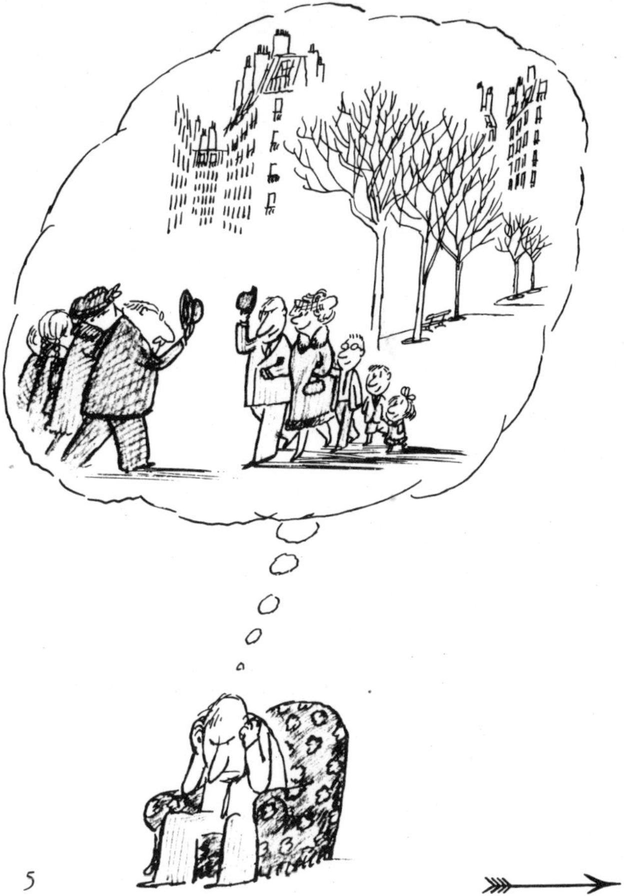

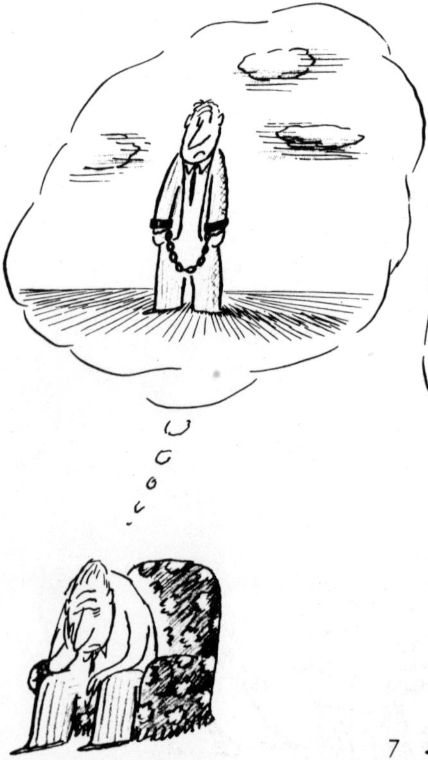

6

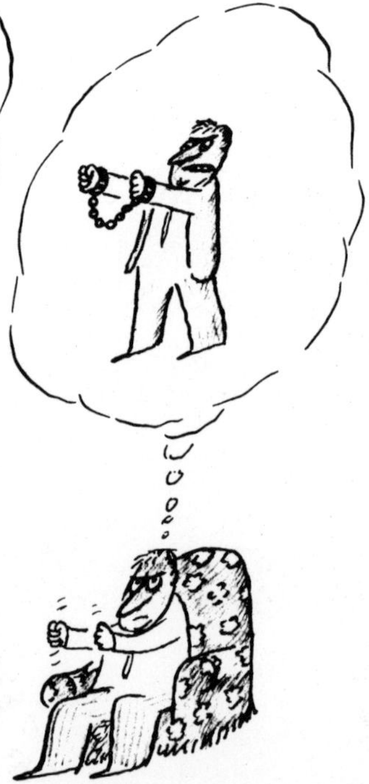

7

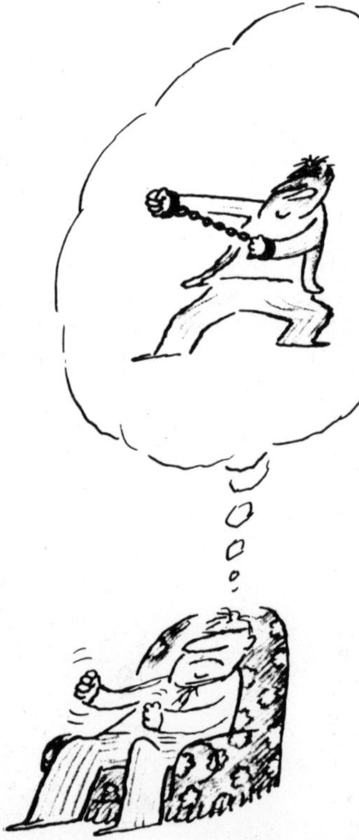

8

9

10

1

2

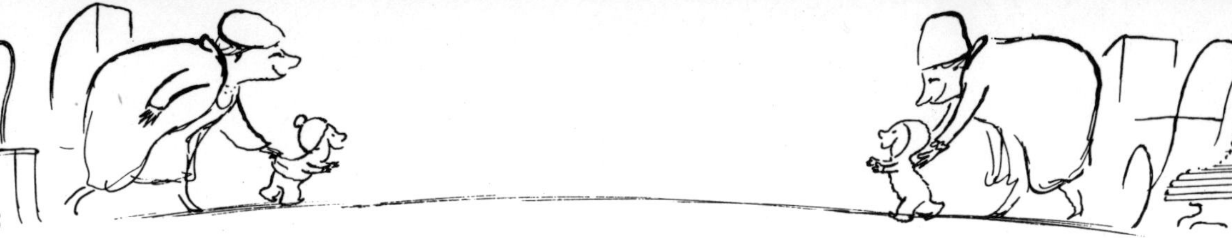

3

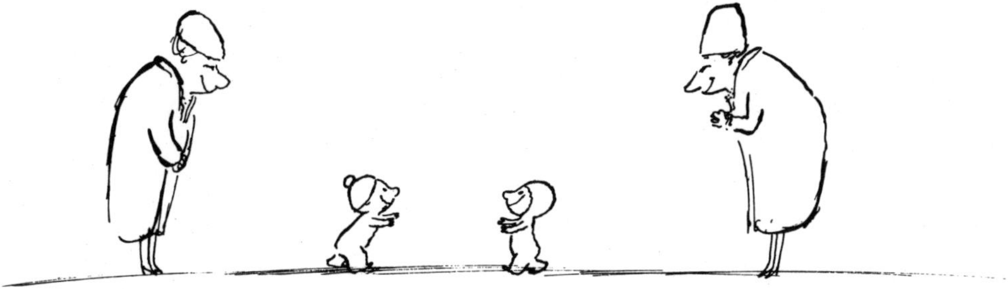

4

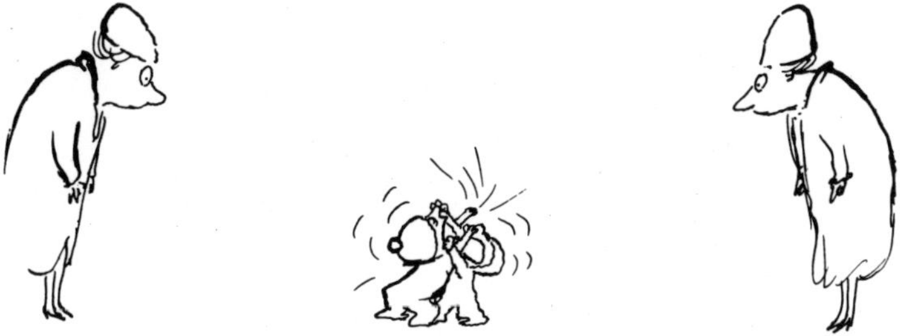

5

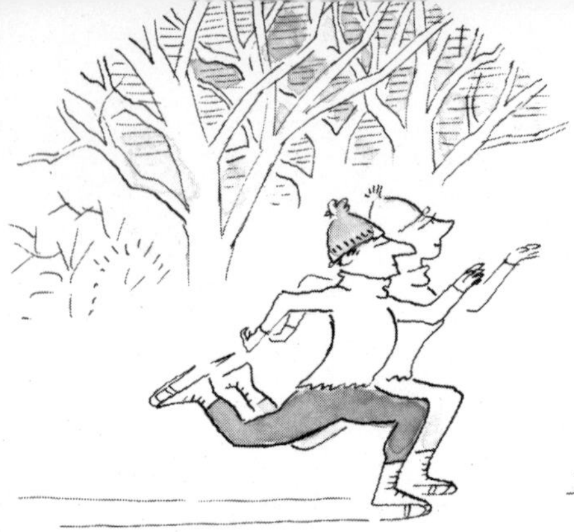

1

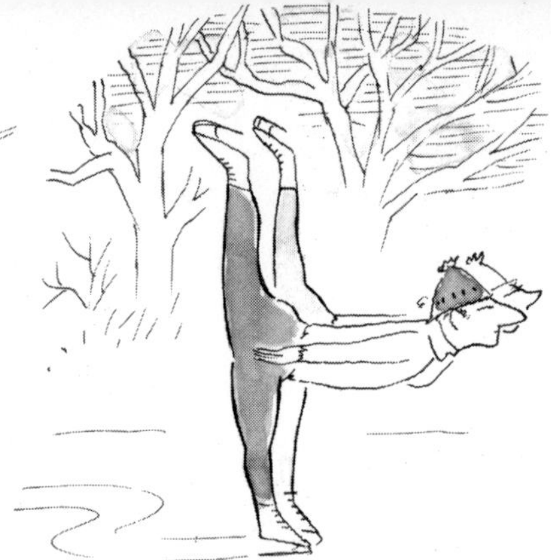

2

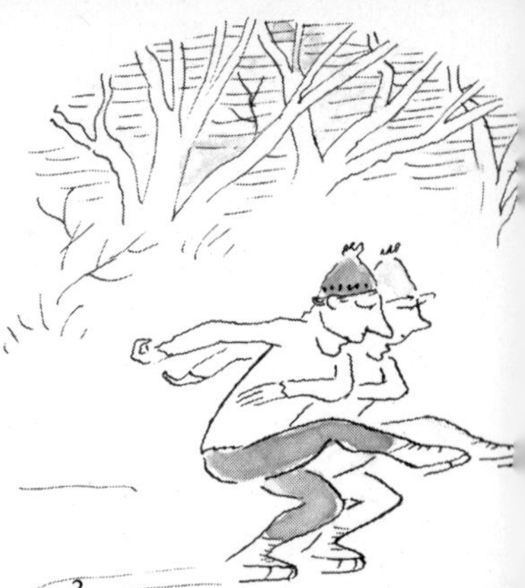

3

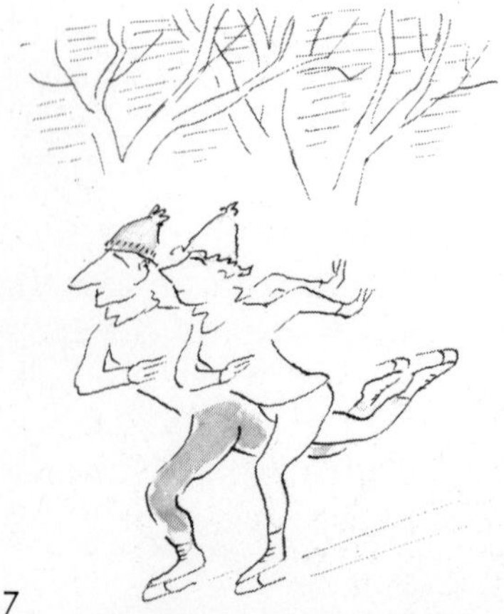

7

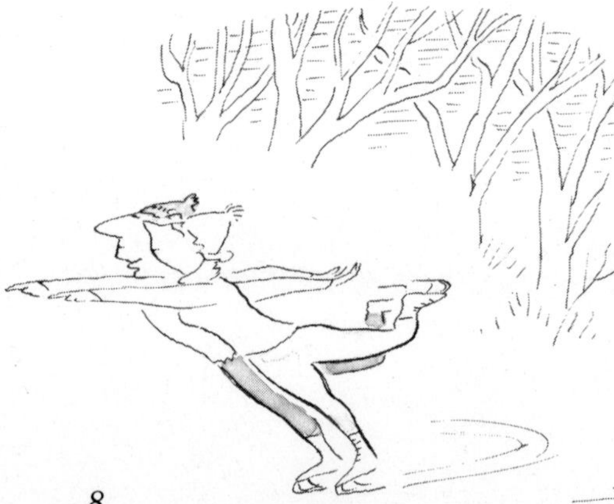

8

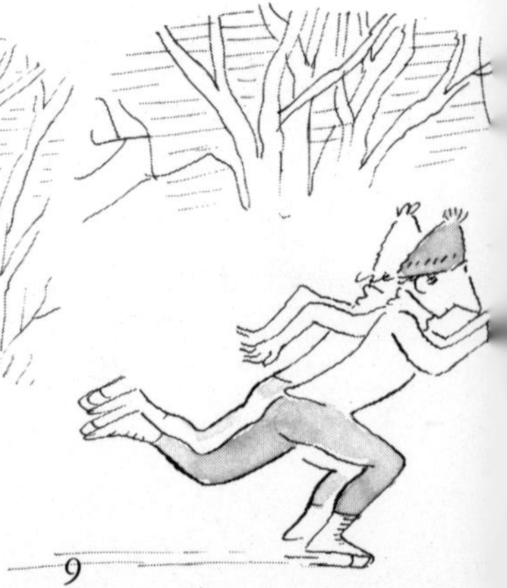

9

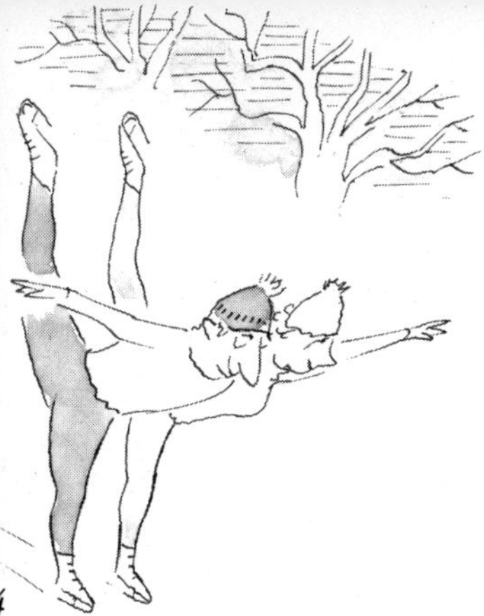

4

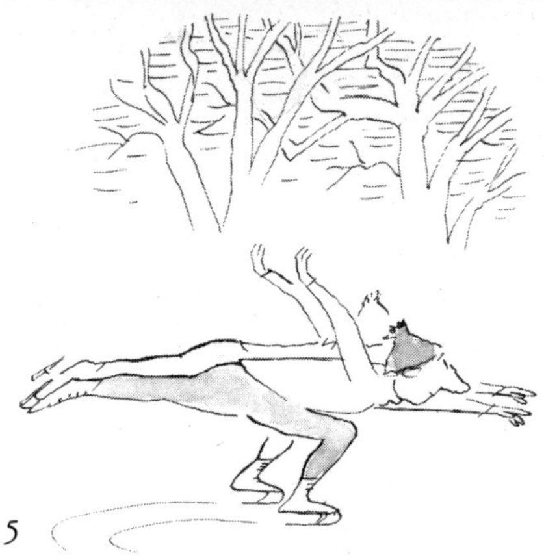

5

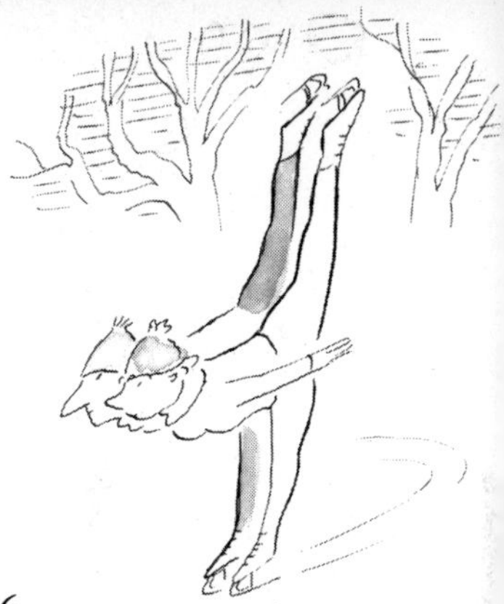

6

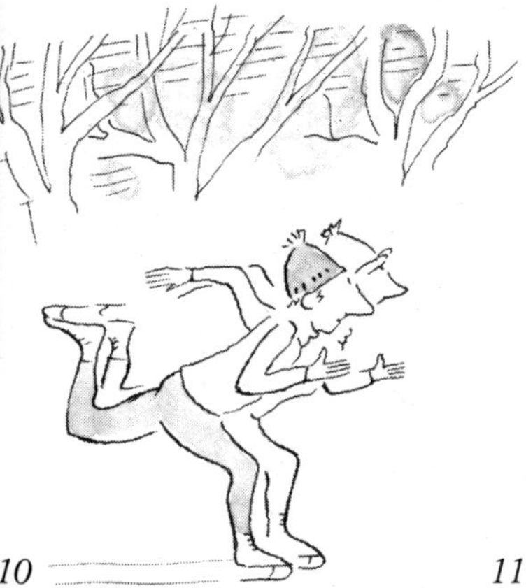

10

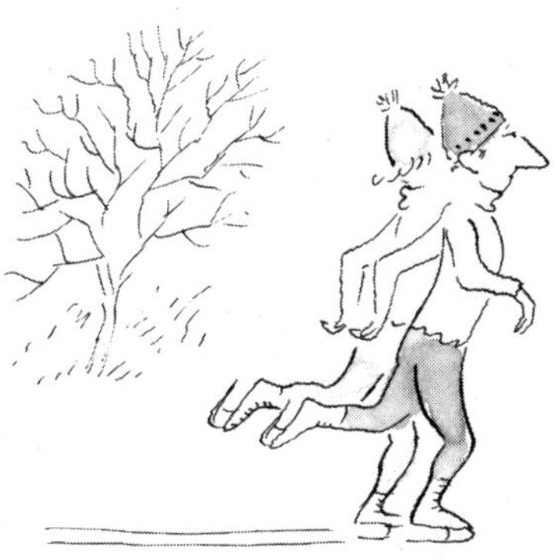

11

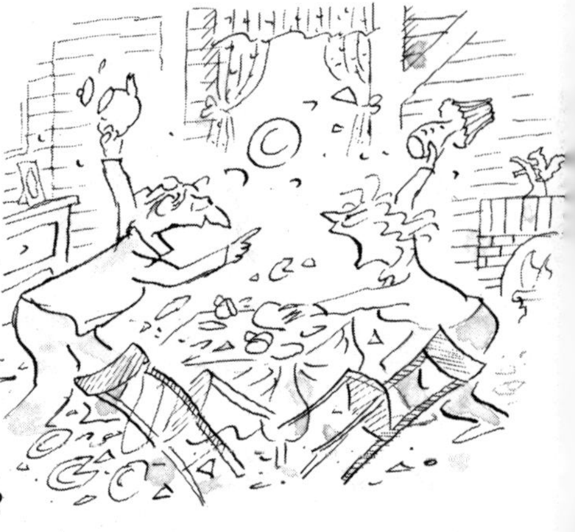

12

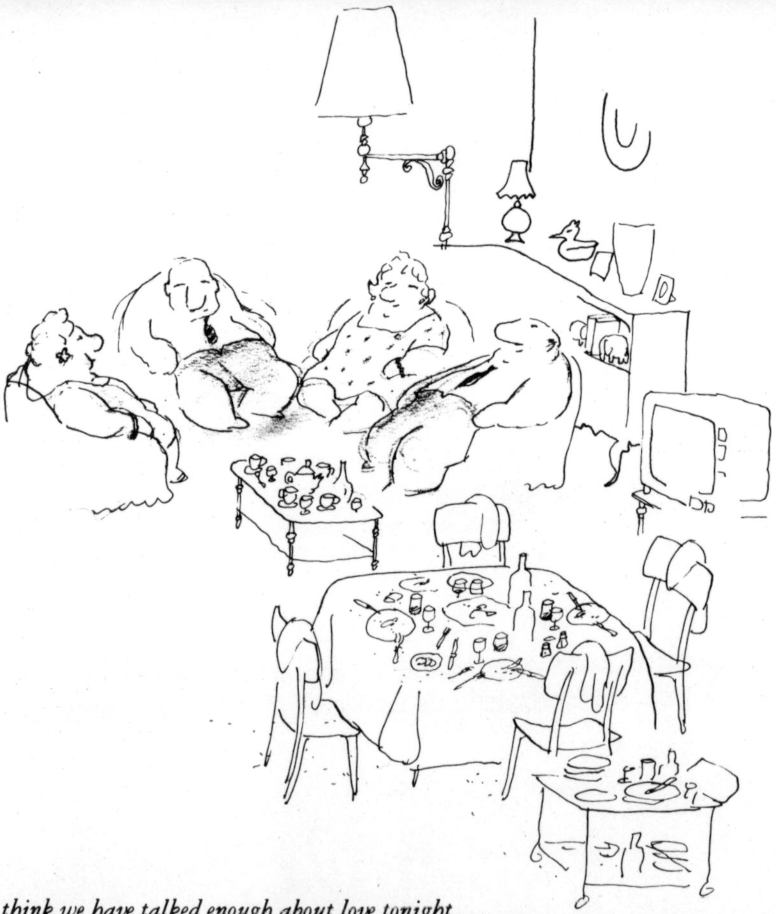

Well, I think we have talked enough about love tonight . . .